The Wilderness Life

The Fesler-Lampert Minnesota Heritage Book Series

This series reprints significant books that enhance our understanding and appreciation of Minnesota and the Upper Midwest. It is supported by the generous assistance of the John K. and Elsie Lampert Fesler Fund and the interest and contribution of Elizabeth P. Fesler and the late David R. Fesler.

The series features works by the following authors:

Clifford and Isabel Ahlgren
J. Arnold Bolz
Walter Havighurst
Helen Hoover
Florence Page Jaques
Evan Jones
Meridel Le Sueur
George Byron Merrick
Grace Lee Nute
Sigurd F. Olson
Charles Edward Russell
Calvin Rutstrum
Timothy Severin
Harold Speakman
Robert Treuer

The following Calvin Rutstrum books are also
available from the University of Minnesota Press

The New Way of the Wilderness
North American Canoe Country
Once upon a Wilderness
Paradise Below Zero
Wilderness Route Finder

CALVIN RUTSTRUM

Illustrations by LES KOUBA

UNIVERSITY OF MINNESOTA PRESS

MINNEAPOLIS

The Wilderness Life

Originally published in hardcover by the Macmillan Company, 1975
Republished by arrangement with Scribner, an imprint of Simon &
Schuster Inc.

First University of Minnesota Press edition, 2004

Published by the University of Minnesota Press
111 Third Avenue South, Suite 290
Minneapolis, MN 55401-2520
http://www.upress.umn.edu

Library of Congress Cataloging-in-Publication Data

Rutstrum, Calvin.
    The wilderness life / Calvin Rustrum ; ill. by Les Kouba.— 1st Uni-
versity of Minnesota Press ed.
        p.   cm. — (The Fesler-Lampert Minnesota heritage book series)
    Originally published: Macmillan Company, 1975.
    ISBN 978-0-8166-4064-5 (pb)
    1. Outdoor life.   2. Camping.   I. Title.   II. Series.
    GV191.6.R87 2004
    796.5—dc22

                                                        2003026562

Printed in the United States of America on acid-free paper

The University of Minnesota is an equal-opportunity educator and
employer.

27 26 25 24 23 22 21   10 9 8 7 6 5 4

Robert Louis Stevenson proclaimed that the success of writing might well depend on having a good amanuensis. On that premise I dedicate this volume to Florence, who labored diligently with these pages while also being my wife and wilderness companion.

Publisher's Note

THE FESLER-LAMPERT Minnesota Heritage Book Series is designed to renew interest in the state's past by bringing significant literary works to the attention of a new audience. Our knowledge and appreciation of the culture and history of the region have advanced considerably since these books were first published, and the attitudes and opinions expressed in them may strike the contemporary reader as inappropriate. These classics have been reprinted in their original form as contributions to the state's literary heritage.

Contents

Contents

Preface: A Prospective Glance

ONCE UPON A WILDERNESS, published in the spring of 1973, was so favorably received by both publisher and reader that I was urged to follow it with another volume in the same general tempo.

It became evident from reader reaction to *Once Upon a Wilderness* that a somewhat philosophic and critical view of wilderness or wildness as a basic concept might make a no less happy book, and one that could include, as well, various human-interest narratives of experience and adventure.

The present volume, *The Wilderness Life,* thus was written with the advantage of already discovered reader appeal. The human-interest narratives are in sufficient variety, I think, for the reader to equate his own position.

The initial chapters discuss the various urban–wilderness dilemmas on the horns of which most of us have been impaled. They should enable the reader to see, in better perspective, the significance of the life experiences in the ensuing chapters.

Most of us have come to discover that wilderness is not some alien interest that we might capriciously regard or disregard. It impinges heavily upon every one of us. Since it is so essential and integral to our whole way of life, even those who existentially hope to adhere strictly to urban life might find in these pages how they also inescapably fit into the complex scheme of the earth's natural environment.

Life everywhere has its basics. They emerge no less in the wilderness, and it is just possible that they become so elemental and revealing under natural conditions as to point the way for an even better urban life. If we have pondered with futility our place in the earth's phenomena, perhaps these pages will help to set us more at ease.

C. R.

1

The Wilderness Point of View

A VAST WILDERNESS sweeps off to the north from my cabin door, across thousands of rockbound wilderness lakes, rivers, and forests, with little interruption for a thousand miles or more. I ask myself, "Is this not too alluring a prospect for activity to be preempted by the writing of these lines?" Had the weather provided a different turn of events this morning, I might have proceeded with this writing another day. Waves on the lake are pounding the nearby shores, hurtling whitewater into the air like inverted cataracts. Rain mixed with hail is pelleted against my window until I wonder why the double-thickness glass does not break. The buffeting wind and thrashing waves impart a basso hissing and booming. Trees sway; some, falling victim to the wind, lose their rooted bond with the earth and strike the ground with what seems crashing despair.

Days such as this are obviously fashioned for contemplation. Yet, earlier in the day, when the elements were reaching their

" . . . to ride out the heavy sea . . . "

most intense bluster, I was leaving the tiny trading post a few miles away with a waterproofed pack of provisions in a canoe, to ride out the heavy sea as one would ride a half-broken bronco. I suppose that leaving the tempestuous lake for the comfort of a cabin was the diversion I needed to get on with this writing. But too long at sedentary work leads one to crave grappling again with the waves, or otherwise flexing one's muscles.

For more than threescore and ten years, I have diligently sought to learn what there is in wildness, or wilderness, whichever term you prefer, that fascinates so many of us, even beyond the multitude of conventional attractions which can truly be said to endure. While it is a great challenge for the adventurer, it also intrigues the cultural mind. The artist tries desperately with his various media to depict it, both realistically and abstractly. The scientist probes its meaning without fully discovering its ultimate secret. Writers of prose and poetry flounder in a nebula of terminology hoping to assess and to convey its values, effects, and grandeur, if not its essential meaning. None of us in some way or place fail to view it with awe if red blood pulses through our veins.

In the daily dialogue of the home and street, no less in some literature, we have observed the phrase, "the best of two worlds." To assume, on this metaphorical basis, that only two exist, would be to involve us, no doubt, in endless controversy of definition. What the phrase implies when I ponder man's attraction to the wilderness is the common distinction between town and country, and in the major generic sense, between the need for a more *natural* rather than a too *artificial* approach toward life.

Viewing both aspects in the current trend, we find that thought on wilderness is changing markedly in recent years, as each of us becomes aware of the absolutely essential need of wilderness for the preservation of human existence. There was a time when we used the term "wilderness" to denote forest, desert, prairie, tundra, mountain, or just a wooded glen. If we sought a dictionary definition for wilderness, we found it listed loosely among such terms as are believed to be synonymous with the boondocks, waste, or wasteland; if used figuratively, it symbolized a bewildering mass. Urbanity became the "thing" and was considered a cultural, orderly process. Early in our history, the wilds were regarded by many as sinful wastes. In those days we had not yet heard the phrase "the asphalt jungle" in reference to the city.

Standard dictionaries and thesauri still labor with derogatory terms for inviolate nature—none to date having fully grasped the significance of wildness or wilderness as life's essence, as generative force. Thoreau proclaimed, "In wildness is the preservation of the world." Abstractions always seem difficult, yet may hold the most profound truths. Wilderness, we finally see in these abstractions, is so intricately a part of our very existence, that were its generative forces momentarily suspended, most of life would wither and die in the interval.

The question often posed is, "How did you happen to get interested in the wilderness?" The question presumes that one has been a product of conventional "propriety" and by some strange quirk in one's character has meddled in an unseemly, eccentric phase of human existence. When so questioned, one might be tempted to say, "Wilderness as natural phenomena? Is there anything else?" The question posed has at times even a note of derision, a presumption that the vast category of culturally developed values has been, of circumstantial necessity, existing primarily for the urbanite, and is minimally accessible to the wilderness resident. But that idea is now as outmoded and deceptive as the bustle skirt.

The Wilderness Point of View

We need to be aware of the fact that even "urbanity," as the term was defined earlier, has lost much of its meaning. Cultural opportunities which once were thought to be essentially limited to the urban framework—art, music, literature, science, and the rest—are no longer only urban but currently move with the speed of light into every cranny on earth by the whole of various electronic media.

We come then to the cardinal question and with some assurance of having the capital answer. What environment, the artificial or the natural, will prove more conducive to our acquiring life's greatest cultural values? We are told that "Man, like the chameleon, assimilates to his environment." This may be open to question in degree; but if we subject the urban individual to an environment different from what he has had over a fair length of time, and at the same time offer him leisure, and for cultural diversion a more viable atmosphere to relieve his tensions, we are apt to find him thinking quite differently, and more advantageously.

The proposal made here is not, of course, that the urban population should pack up and head for the suburbs or go farther into the remote, natural areas. If it did, we would no longer have inviolate wilderness areas to enjoy. Realistically—though it may smack a little of arrogance—the appeal has to be to the individual, of course, who is seriously concerned with an optimal determination of his own existence. At the same time, we need to use whatever influence we possess to raise the levels of environmental quality and human opportunity for all.

What seems to be the most valid proposal is that wilderness as a way of life should simply mean that we function subject to the continually amending natural elements which govern us every moment of life, rather than artifically deviate from them in varying degrees to suffer degeneration of spirit and body.

5

The Wilderness Life

Elemental nature, in spite of being highly interfered with by our imposing artifice, nevertheless is pressing in upon each individual every moment of his existence, although in his daily artificial excursion he too often prefers to ignore this fact. He can't run from its effect into the most artificial hiding place and expect to escape, but tends to believe that he can. The basic wilderness creature that he is will be found manifest under his every dress, his cosmetics, and under any formal, artificial pretension to escape his commendably unique and magnificent mammalian place in the natural scheme. Why he seeks this escape so intensely when it can be his finest, most wholesome, existential choice, perplexes intelligent appraisal.

The effect on us of an unnatural environment should not be our only concern. What affects us as much is the burden of material possessions. Weariness and ennui crowd in on an all-possessing materialism. The child wearies of his numerous sophisticated toys, and develops better with less, where his physical and mental tentacles are prompted to reach out for the unknown. The affluent adult needs to discover that he can find regeneration in his escape from gadgetry, from the too often repeated banquet, and even on occasion from the pretentiousness of his mansion. Eating a simple pocket lunch seated on a log beside a mountain stream and spending a night in a down sleeping robe under the stars can give him by contrast inexplicable delight. Or, let him, at least, be under the simpler roof of a rustic cabin to find his truer self. We may take this literally or symbolically, as we choose. The voluptuous will not fail to know the discomforting glut of excessiveness in anything. Obesity that achieves the lean and the hard condition, usually experiences a moment of euphoria for the first time in life. And once this potential for better living is discovered, it is never questioned as a valuable need.

The Wilderness Point of View

If the forces of nature tend in their cyclical fashion to disintegrate all things, reaching even into the copper-lined, concrete coffin in a mausoleum, to reduce both body and sarcophagus to dust and blend them with the elements, what do the forces provide on the regenerative, the plus side?

This question should overwhelm us. Any conceivable answer has to suggest that the integrating rather than the disintegrating forces of nature become the predominant power—the grand phenomenon—using the disintegrating chemical and physical processes "merely" to achieve again and again the end product of natural production. This is ascending nature at work; this should be the complementary aid to man's best efforts.

Whether one lives in an urban area where scarcely a blade of grass grows to refresh the outlook, or deep in the remote, inviolate back country, dispensing with much artifice and conventional gadgetry can be a better way of life, can produce a more wholesome attitude, and can divert one's interest to a broader point of view. A life focused on the potential junk pile and away from the grandeur and benefits of nature must certainly be demeaning and as sterile as the street asphalt. Even the flowering geranium on the window sill can be a tiny flame to keep a warm, wholesome outlook from being wholly extinguished. As someone once said, if you see a flower blooming in the big city, you know what it has gone through.

"A painted ship upon a painted ocean" may seem dead to some, but the artist who paints the ship as he sees it, riding the storm-tossed sea, has at least a wilderness attitude and likely brings some pleasure to the armchair seafarer. The industrial or office captive who goes to the countryside on weekends may basically have a natural outlook, his weekend outings sustaining him through the intervening majority of days when he is a component of the urban machine.

7

The Wilderness Life

I get letters from readers of my books on wilderness themes who scarcely ever see a tree or a sunset. We might wonder at the paradox that the crews and captains for the greatest early explorations of the wilderness were largely drawn from city populations. It was plainly that these urbanites had grasped the wilderness point of view. If this seems difficult to believe, consider that American Indians are preferred to erect the steelwork of skyscrapers. Between structures, many of them return to their own people in scattered reservations or to some remote cabin in the wilderness, although some circumstantially are confined to the urban, residential stall on the asphalt strip, and see little of the natural, most often preferred elemental life of their predecessors. The urban citizen interested in the wilderness is not always the dilettante. Rather, he too may be one confined to the city by unavoidable circumstance, hoping some day to find in the indeterminate pattern of human existence a way of life that is more satisfying. Is there any one of us who does not sneak a look now and then over the wall of convention, wondering how we became urbanely motivated and at what point we chose our destiny?

Before experience can be gained, an empirically-minded youth has to make difficult value-judgments of what his life-style should be. If convention and too early propagation of his kind do not have him by the scruff of the neck, a rarity, then he might have an opportunity to examine his immediate status and hope to make the required judgments. Even then, projections far enough into the future to choose "the best of two worlds" can be his insoluble problem.

On my tape recorder, a rapid-advance knob suggests a rather farfetched and perhaps frightening hypothesis: So equipped in life with a speculative advance mechanism, we could see a few hundred, or even a few thousand, years of the future pass revealingly before our eyes in seconds. We could thus determine what might be of such impermanent value as to merit our least regard and what would seem most durable and most worthy of pursuit. Perhaps the too-protracted aspect of this concept of time becomes a speculative absurdity, but if we could by foresight alone keep the hypothesis within the scope of our own life-spans—or, say, only a few generations hence—we might draw from it a valuable life pattern, or at least discover what are the most durable and significant values.

The cardinal question: What becomes obsolescent too soon for the good of our immediate lives, our own future, and its contribution to the future welfare of others?

Perhaps, to begin with, we would be unwise to grasp anything too firmly which will in a short time dissolve in our hands or lose its significance in our minds. In my youth, material and financial austerity no doubt was present, but strangely I had no imposing or fretful awareness of it. The local, and later the more expansive, natural environment in which I found an abiding pleasure did not demand much of me in either material things or money. What was considered by some to be material splendor did not seem to make the owner splendid.

The sun rose and set in all its glory ever anew each day without financial or material aid. The rain fell on the forest bloom to keep me ceaselessly contemplating its magnificence though no hand cultivated it nor turned any watering spigots. Trails through the wilds, which I had no part in blazing, had been provided by the treading of its forest creatures for ages. I was given twelve breaths of pure, invigorating air every minute at no cost, by the miraculous conversion forces inherent in vegetation. The fuel needed for my tea pail and bannock-baking fire was supplied merely by reaching for it and using an ax to render it fit for my immediate use. The stage for my entertainment was set in the most dramatic style wherever I turned: vast waterfalls fell in spellbinding, thunderous spectacles to amaze, while along the river wildlife played their repertorial parts, though I paid not a single penny for admission.

This was an extraordinary standard of living, the highest I have ever to this day attained. A time came when my income increased sufficiently to permit me to choose my living standard. While strict economy no longer needed to be considered in my choice of life-style, I found that an increased measure of affluence did not add greatly to the life values I had earlier. If money and material advantages appeared in prospect to improve appreciation of a more natural life, they proved illusory in the end. Money did bring me more readily and more often to remote areas, but then I had reached a good share of them often enough before.

A white man asked the backwoods Indian, "Why don't you work at a steady job and save your money so that you can have more leisure time to enjoy life?" The Indian replied, "I enjoy life all the time and have no steady job." Are we inextricably bound up in a pattern?

I am sure that many will find fault with much of this abbreviating economy. Yet, if one can go from rags to riches, or more accurately from austerity to a reasonable affluence, and find that the higher values of life have not drastically improved one's quality of living—but rather, might even have impeded life with a quantity of goods—then could we not find great merit in getting off the industrial treadmill long enough to appraise our own situation? At least, we might learn why we are driving the treadmill at a speed that too soon brings diminishing returns.

It must not be presumed that I am unable to attach sentiment to, even perhaps to have a kind of reverence for, something materially fine. But an excess of anything destroys its intrinsic value. A spare paddle lying handy in the bottom of my canoe while I ply the whitecaps is certainly of good utility and will possibly ensure survival. A dozen extra paddles, unless I could readily give them away to those who needed them, would become mere clutter in storage or only have value if chopped up in short pieces as fuel for the next campfire. It is as Thoreau suggested regarding the adage, "a stitch in time saves nine," when he added, "so we take a thousand stitches today to save nine tomorrow." The family caught in a perilous position in a war, finding the need to burn their priceless antique furniture as fuel to keep from freezing, did no doubt have a very painful decision to make, but it must have suggested what was of value to life and what was dispensable.

Can we derive from this an attitude? Should we not approach the elemental needs in life as basic and essential rather than seek a plethora of all things? If we need a cord of wood for fuel, why should we cut twenty cords? The live tree, literally and figuratively, could be a better potential on which to depend. The valuable resource left in the ground and sparingly used could certainly be a better bank account. If we acquire and store beyond need, be it money or things, we are obviously bargaining away our priceless hours of life. The integrating forces of nature and their potential are what we have to depend on, not the deteriorating excrescences we heap on our pile as laudable wealth.

Yesterday, these were the utterances of what were considered prissy conservationists; today, in the sudden perils of our economy, they are the truths that strike painfully to the core of everyone's life.

2

What to Expect

THE YOUNG, or the late to get started, setting out on a wilderness journey, will draw their conclusions of what to expect from their parochial experience, from what they have read, and possibly from other contacts such as television wildlife programs and conversations with the initiated. That they will experience a certain amount of misapprehension as to the actuality and that the challenge may differ widely from what was visualized will often become apparent.

The initial trip might be moderated to an advantage. Too major an undertaking at the start can become discouraging. When first I undertook to set up a wilderness program in two prominent, privately owned youth camps, I made the mistake which is best described by the cumbersome term "supererogation"; that is, I overplayed my part. The camps—one for boys, the other for girls—being affluent, I was allowed to purchase large amounts of expensive camp equipment, hire a staff of guides, and generally make the big play. What I soon discovered was that a number of the youngsters did not have to be taken into the remote wilderness areas of the continent, but found high adventure merely by sleeping in a tent fifty feet behind their modern camp cabins on a clear night with the moon shining through the pines. When the next step, sleeping in the tent through a night of rain and awakening in the morning in a wet camp area, was added to their experience, they were on their way to believing that living in the wilds with its adversities was within their province, and they were eager for the greater, more variable, wilderness experience.

A friend of mine, who had previously made a wilderness trip of short duration, decided to take his bride on a honeymoon camping trip. The warm, bright, sunshiny day of departure suggested a week of idyllic weather. Camp was pitched under a clear sky. The following morning a cold rain driven by a high wind was thrashing through the forest, blowing the lake into whitecaps. Disillusionment had intruded upon the connubial tent.

Even weekenders bent on canoe trips down local rivers often start out optimistically in fair weather only to be drenched by rain. So great is this optimism about weather that food is generally carried only in paper cartons, soon to be flattened by the rain, becoming a soggy mess in the bottom of the canoe. Trips frequently start out early in the spring under warm conditions and end up in unseasonable snowstorms, where clothing and equipment are inadequate, and at times actually hazardous.

Perhaps, the psychology here is that we as humans find it extremely difficult to understand the alternate condition when the immediate condition, whatever it is, prevails. As I have pointed out in my book *Paradise Below Zero* (published by The Macmillan Company), it is almost impossible to realize while we are comfortably ensconced indoors that two miles of vigorous hiking in sub-zero weather, with proper clothing, will result in a physical and mental state in which we are very comfortable and are truly enjoying the sub-zero temperatures.

Prolonged rain tends to put some people into a mood in which they have the feeling that sunny weather exists only in some unforeseen future. On one trip I made in the Canadian wild, it rained sometime during every day of twenty-nine days, with no relief except for intermittent overcast skies. When the sun finally did break through, the effect was nothing short of startling. In a later year I made a canoe trip through that same region for seven weeks, and most of the time I was apprehensive over the hazard of forest fires, the weather being so dry.

What we need to consider, of course, whether we are living in the wilderness or in a metropolitan center, is that while life may seem to continue in the norm, it can suddenly turn up a series of anomalies, if not tragedies. If we despairingly assume, as one philosopher did, that pain is the normal state, then we will certainly be surprised to find some joyous periods in the average lives of most of us. To assume that the normal state of a wilderness journey is perpetual pleasure, will, we can be sure, provide its share of disillusionment.

What to expect in turning toward wilderness activity is dependent on how competently we are able to meet average obstacles anywhere with the least difficulty. We need to assume a philosophic attitude toward solutions as well as to use skill.

Capability is not always a matter of age or long experience. I find after working ten years with youth counselors that many of the young do an admirable job of meeting fortuitous problems of life. The youthful outlook is one that is not, of course, easily discouraged—a great initial asset. A lack of empirical knowledge may be a handicap in some instances, but often courage and good judgment carry the inexperienced over many unpredictable hurdles. Judgment is quite often, with the young under stress, coupled with a faculty for ingenuity. It is important, of course, not to presume that this is always so, or that spontaneous youth normally lives with an advantage over experience.

What can the elderly expect to find in retirement to the wilderness? Sometimes I wonder if the slogan, "Old soldiers never die—they just fade away," should not better apply to men of long residence in the wilds. I vividly recall one instance of an old-timer in the Smoky Mountains. He had been in these mountains most of his life. When we had finished discussing the generalities that go with a first contact, he straightened up, and asked proudly, "Wudja like to see my quattas?" The quarters were a tiny, one-room, wooden shack made from weathered, unpainted boards, set picturesquely on a narrow, fast-running mountain stream. Inside he had a wood-burning cook stove, a cot, a small table, two wooden boxes for seats, a homemade rocking chair, and sundries that included some guns and fishing tackle. One whole wall was stacked to the ceiling with neatly piled hardwood splits, all the same length, fuel for the kitchen stove. The old-timer pointed out that the wall of wood was "handy in case of a sick spell." He was ninety-four. His only immediate problem in life was that he had run out of coffee. It was during that period of the Second World War when coffee was rationed. With some coffee ration tokens I had accumulated, I bought several pounds of his favorite coffee for him. Can happiness glow on the face of a man ninety-four? It did. He seemed magnificently adjusted to his environment. Could we but say the same for all of us, wherever we are and at whatever age!

"He seemed magnificently adjusted to his environment."

What to Expect

It should be apparent, therefore, that apprehensions of youthful inexperience or old age, qualms common to the uninitiated, should not prevent anyone from enjoying wilderness. This may suggest living dangerously, but I think the hazards, as judged by what we learn from the news media, are comparatively fewer in the wilds than anywhere else.

The music master's advice to his aspiring concert violin student, "Go home and practice ten years, then come back and we will see how you are getting along," might be construed as a principle for musical achievement, although it certainly was bad psychologically. Hope of success lies more immediate in the evolutionary potential. It is even better to feel that success is just around the corner, and if not the next, then at least around some unexpected corner, than to presume that achievement, no matter what, belongs only to the prodigious or the long-enduring.

In expectation of wilderness living, we can certainly derive pleasure while we are learning and adjusting. Pitching a tent, swinging an ax, baking a bannock in a frypan before an open fire, and a dozen other camp functions can be practiced profitably in an urban backyard, if they are done by the best-known methods and with a zest for learning.

I once entered the wilderness for several weeks with one of the nation's finest hotel cooks, whose wilderness experience from long urban life was, as I chided him, less than zero. A single day of instruction in the handling of various kinds of fires and in the properties of particular wood fuels was enough so that where preparation of food over these fires was concerned, he literally took it away from me. And he went further. He adapted the various fires, flames, or glowing embers to particular kinds of accomplished cooking so readily that I became the eager learner of campfire cooking instead of the teacher. An aspiring wilderness traveler might even try cooking a number of meals on the kitchen range to achieve much valuable practice.

In a rather long lifetime with wilderness companions, I have come to look for innate or potential abilities. Some of the companions I asked to accompany me seemed to have two main qualities which prompted my inviting them: they were enjoyable individuals to be with, and they seemed to have—though without much exercise of them—good physical reflexes. I did not expect them at the start to hold up their end of the camp and travel duties beyond what they could manage from a knowledge growing day to day and from their desire to help. But when a companion appeared interested in performing one of the various camp functions on his own, it was a pleasure to note his reaction when he was left wholly to his own resourcefulness.

Reading books on wilderness adventure, or even books on method, to determine what the wilderness is like, might cause one to suffer delusion. This preparation is, nevertheless, important. We live and learn much by contrasts, and wherever and whenever we can contrast our own empirical or theoretical knowledge with the background we find in the experience and theories of others, we wind up with a result that, at least, has been processed by our own viewpoint, and that is what we have to live with for the time being.

In theory it is very much like a problem in celestial navigation. You don't know exactly where you are but you roughly presume a basic position in your mathematical formula from which you will compute a position. The difference between these positions is called an "intercept"—a correcting value from your original presumption.

Gaining experience is much like that. Your knowledge and that which has been preconceived for your benefit by others has an intercept. It can tell you to move either toward or away from your notion of what a certain thing should be.

Preconceptions also have a strangeness about them when realities are superimposed on them. For example, a map allows one to see a canoe route or a land route in its entirety—the plotted shapes of lakes and land masses easily delineated. In reality, when one arrives on them, they assume a wholly different and confusing aspect, because one's view then encompasses only a mere fragment of the whole land or water area. (See my book, *The Wilderness Route Finder,* published by The Macmillan Company.)

Perhaps as important in the final analysis of what to expect from wilderness is the romantic and aesthetic. But here there is much valid free play of the imagination, and seldom disappointment. If the evening sun breaking across the wooded hills turns the wilderness waters into a fantastically impressive lake of gold to overwhelm you; if at the same time the lone, long-drawn-out, echoing call of a loon nearby is answered miles away to lift your feelings further in unexplainable ecstacy, does it really matter what pleasure you expected? You will inevitably be enthralled.

3

Man Against the Wilderness

THE TITLE OF this chapter might suggest two distinct categories: persons who have a strong affinity for wilderness values and those who presume to be artificially apart from nature with a prerogative for manipulating natural values chiefly for utilitarian purposes. Neither is purported here to be the whole answer.

The suggestion that man is but one species of the animal kingdom seems to give him trouble. If we can view him on a spectrum of his evolution, attributing to him a remarkable primordial nature on the left, he obviously tries to bear defensively to the right. Wilderness has become something he holds alien—not a magnificent process with which he should be in accord. For him to identify with wilderness as an ecological component often leaves him disturbed. Groomed, dressed, housed, and utilitarian, he chooses largely to remain aloof from the ecology that inextricably links him with all other organisms. The farther from his biological kinship he can remove himself, the more intellectual and civilized he has regarded himself throughout history, the more he believes himself to rise above all other biological phenomena.

The indictment, of course, notes the exception; and we can be encouraged that his number is growing rapidly.

It might be too soon to expect that man will be ecologically elated over the miracle of his mammalian self and revel in the fact that he has emanated, as have all creatures, from basic wilderness origins. We can, nevertheless, see a growing evidence of the discovery that any refinement in our presumed civilization, any great erudition attached to industrial science, art, utilitarianism, and other achievement, must by comparison shrink in the face of our sensitivity to nature. We have been reminded through the years that art and most culture which endures depend on simplicity—not that simplicity, we are told, which is a euphemism for folly, but the simplicity of truly noble minds.

We can now presume from overwhelming scientific evidence that the wilderness nature of man is such that he cannot survive detached from a sound ecology. Can we presume on this premise that he will take full advantage of his discovery soon enough? If he can, it might be interesting to speculate on what terms a viably stable civilization could come about.

To begin with, we cannot presume that man will again enjoy a period in history comparable to that when the population was small enough to make the least harmful inroads on the environment. Nor can we presume that he will ever become so consigned to nature that he will not require the amenities of an advanced technology. He may by some compelling circumstance have to return in part to the manual processes to supplant some of the machines. But the lever, the wheel, and the computer will, no doubt, always remain, although they may not always have enough of the complement fuel energy required to motivate them fully.

What looms on the horizon most promising in allowing man to continue ecologically in complement with the vibrant earth can be summed up in the word *quality*. If every item produced by the hand of man were required by a new competition and by inspection legislation to be the very best possible in workmanship and quality, most of the problems that relate to our ecological imbalance and that even threaten our existence would tend toward resolution, simply by industry's not having to saturate the market with a vast, overwhelming amount of trash planned for obsolescence. One quality item could replace ten or a hundred planned for obsolescence. This seems too monumental to achieve soon, but it may prove by example to be the inevitable goal.

Most metallic items bought in recent years rust out before they wear out because of poor alloys, and, in turn, wear out long before they should. Repairs and replacement of parts have given way to junking a whole assembly or to purchasing the new replacement planned for obsolescence. Recycling is most commonly frowned upon. It seems to be more convenient to destroy the forests for pulp than to convert yesterday's waste-paper into tomorrow's newsprint, although quality newsprint can be economically attained in the recycled product. Perhaps where wisdom is lacking and avarice is not, we need to supply legislation.

Suppose that manufacturing restrictions on various items were such that they could not fall beneath an optimal quality level. How many industrial chimneys would greatly reduce the spewing out of needless, excessive pollution? How many steel mills could cut the five-day labor grind to less at the same pay and the same company profit? What would it do toward saving our natural areas and prolonging our natural resources? If we applied this same principle to everything we manufactured, what would be the quality of the air in time? A better quality of metal alloys and replacement of small parts could leave most mechanized items so permanent as to make them available to coming generations; whereas now, new and beaming in their coat of enamel, they are in a large measure soon relegated to the junkyard.

Suppose that we could reverse the industrial situation by quality production, so that the natural elements would predominantly freshen urban centers rather than urban industry polluting outlying nature. In short, suppose we so managed our methods that the vast, natural, compensating forces were allowed to work to the advantage of industry and its employment.

Should it happen that the forces of nature will eventually win out against reckless exploitation, the gain obviously will be man's. Nature, inscrutable and impersonal as it is, apparently regards its progeny's learning as the mother regards the child's learning. The bumps and hurts teach.

As bacterial growth, creeping over the culture on which it grows, eventually by multiplicity alone destroys itself, so might humans by reckless propagation risk drastically reducing their number by some yet unknown decimating force.

There is no need for gloom, however, even at the multiple funeral of man's catastrophic mistakes. Great wilderness areas still remain, and certainly the forces of nature will not become static in the restoration process. They continuously move and repair even though man continually ravages. The vandals are loose, but in their wake come nature's engineers to set things right again. When man has reached the ravage point of diminishing returns, nature will ride in on a catch-up course.

23

Unfortunately, at that point there will be a terrifying penalty to pay.

Before the hearth, on the lecture platform, in schools and colleges, the word finally is going round for man to make an adjustment to wilderness—not ravage it. The youth of the world in large numbers are turning their attention to the possibility of a greater life fulfillment. But youth is ephemeral, and the young must exercise their prerogative before time robs them of their youth.

What is astounding today is that a reorientation of intellect has, by virtue of scientific discovery, grasped the indispensable need for wilderness. No longer do we make the grave mistake that only the rustic mind is adaptable to wilderness, the intellectually cultured belonging to the city. No doubt primordial man got a pleasant reaction from wilderness and possessed a certain elemental knowledge about it; but the inner sanctuaries of the wilderness are being opened only by the most assiduous study, research, and exploration. Intellect has found natural phenomena vast and challenging in every department. The man who could not accept a friend's invitation to go abroad at no expense because he had not yet explored his backyard, exemplifies the dilemma of the researching scholar who contemplates the vast wilderness and its complex phenomena as a laboratory.

Those who are penned in by brick, mortar, and asphalt may get only an occasional glimpse of nature, but this does not mean that the glimpse has been insignificant. A cosmos revolves within a drop of water. The cultured individual does not suffer a serious inadequacy for thought and understanding because he has no immediate access to a whole mountain, a blazing sunset, or the Grand Canyon to feed his spirit. On the other hand, he ought to have more than the ephemeral bloom in a florist shop and a patch of sky between buildings.

Man Against the Wilderness

After any degree of association with wilderness, we do not necessarily conjure up some individual fact, sight, action, sound, or spectacle in the wilds most salient in memory. The digital computer awes us with its input capacity, only to look crude by comparison with the input of the human brain exposed to nature. Once in the wilderness a vast complexity of impressions is gained, perhaps none particularly obvious to our senses at the time, but all feeding back to intensify our interest.

To maintain himself as integral with nature and still keep a strong hold on artificiality has been man's problem. To regard ourselves as emanating from the earth as just one more living form, complex in our biology, would give us too little to exalt our conventional stature. We had to contrive much artificiality for our distinction. But how needless. Our species, like the proverbial lily, does not have to be gilded.

Is it any wonder then that so many scorn wilderness as a pattern in which we are inextricably an integral part?

A power company, strange as this recent transition has become, advertised, in its desire to be ecologically cooperative, "If we call nature our mother, then every living thing on this earth is our brother." This thought is disturbing to many people.

Man, capable of contriving industrially far beyond any other creature, has not fully escaped the basic concept that we are at the same time integral with wilderness. Industry, of course, has not proven to be man's paramount civilizing process. Some industry of an extraordinary kind is carried on by the so-called lower animals. Beaver build dams and birds build nests with fantastic skill and design. Spiders spin webs to capture their food supply, the support principle and positional advantage amazingly contrived. A species of wasp digs holes in the ground for pupae incubation and food storage, refills the hole, and then uses a stone to tamp and pack the earth—something I could not believe until I saw it done. Gulls pick up mussels and fly to suitably high altitudes to drop them and break the shells, in order to get at the meat. Migratory birds navigate the skies with incredible direction-finding processes that are yet beyond man's present understanding and beyond his capability without instruments and study.

The comparison may prove nothing, but it is not odious. What it emphasizes is our integral position with wilderness, and the futility of our too common desire to assume a position apart from and against wilderness.

We are not aliens contemplating nature; we are nature. We might assume the urban role and remain there, with an abiding faith and feeling that in its confines we can hide from natural realities; but nature will walk through walls of concrete, glass, and steel without opening a single door and still control our every function and our destiny. In all of us, in every plant and raindrop there is that integrating or disintegrating, illimitable force.

To awake in the freshness of morning and know that one is a part of the rising sun, the orange-tinted fog, the vibrant earth, the magnificence of growth, is to discover an affinity that comes closer to life's fulfillment than any other. There is a confidence that no matter how inscrutable life is, we can rest our case with nature.

In *Candide* it was hinted that the secret of happiness was simply to keep on hoeing one's garden. The figurative advice here may be a bit deceptive or too metaphoric, but we can, at least, gather from it that we shall never get quickly to the nucleus of the happiness riddle. Expecting to escape from urban routine living to some preconceived natural paradise where bliss

"Beaver build dams . . ."

is the order of each day can be our greatest single illusion. We need a mode, a plan to go with our dream.

Wilderness as a way of life assumed early is obviously the best means to the desired end. We, of course, have this transition problem especially where retirement is contemplated. It has been suggested that the phrase "retirement from" ought never be used, but rather "retirement to," since the central nervous system will not allow the human physical and mental machine, if we may call it that, to be suddenly turned off from its long operation, without it suffering from the corrosion of disuse. Retirement needs best be to a retooling of interest, as it were, for a whole new motivation in continuing life's progress.

If we need a formula for making the change, the best one seems to be the gradual development of an avocation, a hobby, or some other time-absorbing diversion which will eventually usurp our regular vocation. We can then aspire to that para-doxical luxury of finally being too busy to indulge time on a commercial job.

Industry and business could logically be the best media for developing this transition from work to hobby. Instead of abruptly retiring people at a certain age, the retirement might be an attenuating process where employment days became fewer each year. The number of days worked per week might be reduced in inverse proportion to the number of years employed. It will be quite obvious on this plan that as leisure is gradually released to the individual, he will as gradually find a diversionary need for it.

So habit-forming are we that a large percentage of the retired seek jobs to fill the newly acquired leisure time. This is chiefly due to the difficulty of not knowing how to cope with the grand opportunity of leisure, whether because of a want of interests or a want of money to support their interests. The frame of life leading to retirement has been one that rests too much on the brick and mortar standard of metropolitan life, where value is generally translated into cost; where daily tasks, however small, have to be done by others. A vast number of people, on retirement to a more natural environment, would be doing many things themselves, to great personal advantage, which ordinarily in the city they would feel obliged to have others do for them at a big drain on their retirement income. The therapeutic value of performing these many routine tasks themselves is inestimable, since on retirement there is often a tendency to assume a phlegmatic existence, almost akin to invalidism.

What we tend to overlook in this regard is that retirement, or leisure of any kind, should not be viewed as a form of abandonment, but as a way of assuming various new responsibilities.

4

As a Way of Life

THERE IS LITTLE DOUBT that for contrast we need to live away from urban centers for a while, as Thoreau suggests, in order to learn what are the greatest human needs. On the same premise, the individual who tends to shun crowded society might move to advantage for a time among the excessively gregarious in order to learn from society's dense population what profitably could be included and what might well be deleted in the leisure of more remote living.

If in our self-appraisal we feel most secure in the crowd, we might consider whether we are not simply "running aimlessly with the populace" and have failed to discover that any commendably creative life requires a certain amount of self-sustaining isolation. At the same time, we need to recognize that hermits we are not, and if we literally attempt to get away from it all, in time we may come to realize that without a wise modification of our living habits, we may be trying to sustain what can prove to be a vacuous individualism.

The suggestion that we actually can get away from it all by some diversionary tactic intrigues but does not wholly convince. That most of us at one time or another have speculated on that possibility is, of course, safe to say. What it involves might be worth considering.

There seems to be little doubt at this stage of psychoanalytical research that we, meaning just about all of us, are highly gregarious—if not inescapably an integral part of the madding crowd, then certainly incapable of wholly parting from it. The strange aspect of this is that the need to be near others may not be one entirely of practical necessity, although this is obviously a part of it, but rather an innate compelling force to which we can attach any meaning we wish that resolves our own individual compulsion to be with others.

Wherever we find an individual living entirely alone in the wilderness, it is usually for a limited time—occupations such as trapping or prospecting or specialized private or governmental pursuits may require it. Even in these pursuits, a time comes when human contact becomes the cardinal need, though this may have to be deferred on occasion by some compelling circumstance.

Now and then one finds the individual who expresses a strong disdain for society and presumes that life alone in a wilderness cabin far removed from human contact will be nirvana. What we have to consider in his favor, in spite of our gregariousness, is that being entirely alone in a wilderness solitude for a period can be an experience offering pleasure more exquisite, more revealing than is possibly conceivable by those who have never wandered away from the crowd. Every element becomes more intimate, more sharply focused, more flavorful, a bit more understandable in the light of an artful simplicity. Recent psychological experiments have shown an extraordinary learning process achieved by those who have voluntarily undergone solitary confinement for certain periods. The introspection ability discovered was amazing.

If the period of isolation in the wilderness is long enough, one can develop, to borrow a phrase, a "territorial imperative"—a passion for possessing the immediate environment which is so strong that encroachment upon the area by anyone can stir up utter resentment. A stranger, or even an acquaintance, intruding on the scene is felt to be a trespasser.

In time that changes. A lone canoeist coming upon the beach, a winter traveler drawing a toboggan, or even a snowmobile driver, stopping the raucous sound of his vehicle to warm up, can become so welcome as to offer a dramatic moment of pleasure. After long travel alone with canoe, dogsled, packhorse, or backpack, I have come upon trappers, mining prospectors, mountaineers, and others deep in the wilderness, and found that we would rather sit before an open fire, talk, and feast all night than sleep.

Suffice it to say that the majority of people, regardless of income, position, domestic circumstance, advantage or disadvantage, have, no doubt, thought that some place and condition might offer a better life-style, idealistically—one that offered at least increased peace and contentment. But nirvana there is not.

The decision actually to make the move involves as much a matter of what you need to take with you as what you thought to escape.

Many seeming indispensables in the final resolution of a reasonably successful escape plan often do prove dispensable without regret. In planning to try a wilderness life in a cabin on the shore of that most beautiful lake in the world, on a mountain stream where rainbow trout leap in the sunlit pools, on a wild seashore, or even on the sun-splashed desert, we are faced, of course, with realistically considering, to the best of our ability, each factor impinging on life as it has been and by comparison as it will be upon fully making the change. In the process we will likely have the pleasant surprise that a disturbingly complex life was left behind for a simpler, more healthful and serene one.

A substantial part of my mail comes from readers who seek some kind of wilderness life, essentially life in a simple cabin. Most are concerned with two particular phases: Can they dare to build their own cabins themselves, manually, and can they maintain a wilderness life without having had more than a casual acquaintance with the wilds?

The chief factor they need, I find important to convey, is the initiative to try. Those who do, usually succeed. Some have succeeded so admirably, I am even flattered that they chose to get my opinion in the first place. Those with a prodigious ability to carry out their programs occasionally supply answers to some of my own questions. One of the most interesting manifestations is the originality in cabin style to fit the change in life-style—a radical deviation from the conventional and at times a reversion to what we once considered pioneer life.

During the decade and more that my book *The Wilderness Cabin* (The Macmillan Company) has been available, I have been receiving reader correspondence that helps me to keep a finger on the pulse of this interest in wilderness living. The last few years show a surprising increase in interest. Since cabin building is extensively covered in that volume, I need only refer briefly to what seems essential to the theme of this chapter.

Most of us will draw a rather definite conclusion as to the extent of our individual needs for remoteness. My own is that we have a greater chance of success with wilderness life if we settle on the perimeter of the wild rather than too deep into it.

If this seems to suggest a compromise between urbanity and the primordial, it admittedly does that. In my early wilderness days, we talked about the "jumping-off place" to the wilderness, not the "point of departure." Perhaps it would not seem bizarre to suggest that the perimeter is the jumping-off place to both wilderness and city.

But when we speak of the perimeter, we are confronted with the need for a definition of what that specifically is. If we can provide a reasonably well-delineated line of demarcation, we are faced with determining how wide that line will be. Earlier in wilderness life over the continent, that line was narrow. It was black and critically defined between wilderness and settlement. Now the line tends to be grey and diffused. The diffusion lies in the words "communication" and "transportation."

If the cabin can be reached by car, obviously the grey will be closer to the white or traffic-infested margin of the line than to the black, unless a narrow road sign reads "dead end."

We can, of course, have access to any wilderness area by air, where planes are not banned, if we have a budget that will allow about two dollars per mile for air travel.

The determination of a site is not easy. Most particularly there is the matter of the individual's income and occupation, if any. The five-day week and the two-week vacation, compounded with a possible gasoline shortage, place the site where it has to be accessible for those limited periods. The affluent who cannot afford to tear themselves away any longer than weekends are in the same time-limited category, of course. The retired, the so-called idle rich, those who can find employment on the wilderness perimeter, the mail-order craftsman or artist, the government employee connected with wilderness matters, the prospector, and various others will naturally have to select the most practical and desirable site largely on the immediacy of their specialized needs.

When my wife and I searched for a site it had to be based on what a writer's needs would involve. A writer on wilderness quite obviously, it would seem, requires an immediate wilderness as a laboratory. But that could be considered a moot question. It might be well, for example, to turn one's face toward a blank wall in order to allow the imagination to have full play without distraction. One does not necessarily write about the wilderness by looking out upon it from a grand view studio and reading it off as one would the notes of music. The brain, a miniaturized computer, collects input over a long period, in numerous ways, the total being scrambled in such a fashion that the feedback eventually brings a desired and orderly result.

What my wife and I learned, after having been crowded out of previous cabin locations by the incursion of growing populations, was that our retreat could be only to another wilderness perimeter, not too deep into the wilds.

My publisher and people who read my books purport to have some sort of a claim on me. They want their letters answered. This implies a need for mail delivery at reasonable intervals. Anyone accustomed to mail delivery every day would consider our weekly wilderness delivery a serious inconvenience.

Twenty-five miles from an automobile road and two miles by canoe from a flagstop on a Canadian railroad that runs through a wilderness held the best advantages for us. If one needs redundancy of transportation in a situation like this, it is so readily available one can almost indulge a capriciousness of choice. There is the canoe and paddle, or canoe and outboard motor, with a few intervening portages to the outside world. There are airplane bases to call for a charter by radio telephone. If the spring thaw or the early winter freezeup prevents a plane

"Wildlife will spill over in varying degree to your very door."

landing in front of the cabin, one can use a radio telephone to call for a helicopter that will, for an extra charge, snatch one out of almost any open wilderness spot or even from the precariously thin shore ice. In winter after the heavy freeze, there are the ski-equipped plane and the snowmobile.

Living on the wilderness perimeter, you will discover that wildlife will spill over in varying degree to your very shore and door.

The individual seeking to isolate himself completely deep in the wilds over long periods will likely find in his pursuit of isolation that he has to forgo too many utilitarian and social advantages. On occasion, the rare hermit-like individual is found paradoxically carrying on life permanently in some faraway wilderness area; but he is the extreme, so much so that he tends to become newsworthy.

In a lifetime of travel and living in the wilderness through about half of each year, I have met the rare hermit here and there. However, I haven't known any among them who were what might be considered *absolute* hermits—any who, for example, were not overjoyed at the sight of another human being, though they gave the impression that it was a common event. After you have spent days with such an individual and are about to leave, you do not have to be capable of penetrating your host's thoughts intuitively to guess that he will sink into the slough of lonely despond for several days after your departure. His composure and his resignation to solitude are usually recovered, if once he had them; but a visitor can be a form of social contamination causing the deep wilderness dweller, unable to shake his loneliness malady, to seek a change of residence to the wilderness perimeter.

The individual who pretends to scorn his own kind and builds a cabin deep in the wilds to prove the need for isolation, will, ironically enough, be seen visiting on the perimeter with methodical frequency, even though he continues his residence deep in the wilderness. In time he, too, most likely will rebuild his cabin on the perimeter. He now has what fulfils his needs —a chance to enjoy remoteness deep in the wilds when the mood strikes him, but always with the diversion which the permanent perimeter dwelling holds out. After protracted periods in a remote wilderness, one such cabin dweller told me that without provocation he would, now and then, step outside his cabin "to see if anybody was coming," though he knew the chances of seeing anybody were extremely slim in that isolated place.

Man and woman living together in a remote wilderness cabin manage the most consistently stable isolation, although the time comes when the woman needs "woman talk," and the man needs "man talk." Wilderness dwellers fare best in the woman-man combination. I have been told that a woman's nature makes her more of an exhibitionist than is man; but strut does the cock as well, and if the woman does need a kind of social exposure not equally attributable to the man, then she should have it, and who shall say that women do not well play the role to men's satisfaction?

Some among the populace, considering a transition from city to country or wilderness perimeter living, have apprehensions that in the urban bustle there will be activities which leave them out of the swim of things. It is not a notion of missing the grand performance, or whatever the single event. These, when the occasions occur, they will attend. It is simply a matter of their feeling disassociated from the crowd. When the change from city to country is finally made, they discover that remoteness from whatever they desired was largely illusory. It becomes possible, as they see, actually to have one hand on the natural environment, and with the other to reach for people or anything they consider urbanly desirable.

What is brought to the home in the city or town by radio, television, and telephone, can in most instances be brought to the wilderness perimeter cabin. And there is almost a certainty that the electronic communication entertainment one is enjoying in the wilderness will be exactly the same as that available to the multitude in the city. Some television and radio sets now on the market can be powered either by battery or utility-transmitted current. In the term "solid state" comes the advantage to the wilderness dweller. It simply means that the equipment no longer has the heavy battery drain of electric current suffered with tubes—these having been replaced with transistors, drawing so little current from the batteries that a set in a radio lasts for months with ordinary use. A television set used where there is no transmitted current can be operated on a twelve-volt storage battery, recharged at selected, noise-tolerable periods with a small, portable, gasoline-driven generator.

What will become apparent to the wilderness dweller is that determination of program and the time spent with radio or television will be quite different, because his whole life-style will change—much more time being spent actively out of doors. So evident is this that wilderness cabin life is occasionally preferred without radio, television, and radio telephone, even where their cost is no object.

Even semi-remoteness once frightened some of those who loved wilderness, because they could not cope with isolation for more than brief periods. Radio telephone systems now leap over vast intervening wilderness areas. Plane bases for charter flights are quite systematically distributed over most wilderness areas of the North American continent, if not over the world. The canoe should, no doubt, be paddled through the silent

"Winter wilderness isolation . . ."

places of the wilderness for greatest enjoyment; but if there is a sudden need for quicker access to the outside, for moving upstream through very fast water, or for getting over large expanses of water against a headwind, there is the outboard motor.

Winter wilderness isolation (a pleasant thought) was once pretty much a reality. Today, one can use the radio telephone and have a ski-equipped plane set down in front of the cabin on the lake ice in less time than one could summon a taxi to take an expectant mother from city suburb to a hospital. The snowmobile can also greatly expedite shopping in winter at some distant post.

To dispense with modernization or to include it in the cabin on the perimeter or deep in the wilderness, therefore, becomes a matter of individual choice. The crux of the choice rests on how much encumbrance and clutter one wants, as against how close to artful simplicity one hopes to live. Perhaps the greatest risk is increasing what we might call convenience, and paying for it with maintenance problems and physical debilitation from lack of exercise.

There is one phase of modernity, however, that seems indispensable: refrigeration. Nothing is more insipid than a warm drink of water. Even in the earliest wilderness life this had prime consideration, and was solved by the traditional ice house. The task of putting up the ice supply each winter for warm weather was no small chore, however. An insulated building and a vast amount of sawdust were required. Today, refrigeration in the wilderness cabin is best solved with the propane gas refrigerator. It seems incredible that only a small flame thermostatically controlled in these units can bring about refrigeration and freezing. Electric refrigerators are also made possible by the installation of a power plant, but here the joy of solitude departs as the frequent noise of its exhaust day and night breaks both solitude and sleep.

Life in the wilderness cabin can, of course, go on even without refrigeration of any kind. It is not available, for example, on extended canoe travel, except on the tundra, where ice is still just below the ground in midsummer. Some cooling of water can be had with a canvas water bag through the process of evaporation. Desiccated, freeze-dried, canned, and dry staple foods need no refrigeration.

Where transportation allows, say, procurement of a weekly supply of food, it would seem needless, if refrigeration were had, not to avail oneself of some fresh items. Milk, if first frozen solid, can be in transit for a whole day in warm weather, and later thawed as needed, without affecting its quality. Cream cannot be so treated. It goes into curd. Cream substitute in powdered form is not too bad.

In the remote wilderness area, fresh food can be supplied by charter plane. The cost is something to consider if the budget has to be watched. But even here, a great enough supply can be flown in to make it pay, especially if, in addition to a refrigerator, one has a propane gas freezer. The advantage of this method is that the time of flight (cruising at about 120 miles per hour) to the average wilderness cabin from a supply center is so short, nothing can spoil en route. It might be said in conclusion then that life in the wilderness can be maintained on nearly the same general level of modernization as that in settled areas, if one so desires. But if a word to the wise is sufficient, keep to that level where wilderness values will predominate *as a way of life.*

5

Security and the Wilderness

THE SUDDEN compelling change today in the tempo of urban life suggests the wisdom of avoiding many of the conventional economic demands that embody extravagance, waste, and voluptuousness. This is possible, of course, to some degree in any environment, urban or other; but it obviously has the greatest chance for realization in the more natural environment, which can vary from regions beyond suburbia to the wilderness fringe, and even deep into the wilderness.

Earlier in colonial history, civilization, surrounded by wilderness, did not reach much beyond the boundaries of a township. Most of what was required could be had from the soil, from the wilds, from village craftsmen, or was often homemade, and whenever possible, things were mended for continued use. On occasion, skills and employment were cooperatively traded. Inherent in this parochial life was an element of self-sustaining economic security. Populations being small, they made no serious drain on the immediate resources.

As transportation improved and spread, demands for goods grew. The luxuries of yesterday became the necessities of today. As exotic and processed food imports increased in the community, they were soon assimilated by a more luxurious standard, finally being regarded as common staples. Home gardens tended to disappear. For centuries the rapidly accelerating pace of supplying processed foods and gadgets drew only common praise. Industrial saturation, it was believed, could do no harm. Competition was yet to become an abusive contest of business survival, although it was heading in that direction. If there was concern about a rapidly increasing population, industry and the pulpit proclaimed the dire need for reproduction; the greater the population, the better for business. It was believed, if considered at all, that this luxury-expanding, material-depleting behavior pattern of society could affect us only beneficially. If ecologically it seemed damaging to the environment or too resource-consuming, it would soon be resolved, we were told, by the replacement magic of technology.

We have now been made aware of the gravity of this delusion.

The suddenly discovered shortage of fuel energy sources today threatens to create a serious economic deprivation, ramified into material shortages of all commodities. Thus, for the first time in history outside of war, we are all confronted with the imperative need to change, perhaps permanently, our whole life style. Recycling, salvaging, repairing, and mending are now becoming not only good policy but an urgent necessity.

Security? Life in the early wilderness colonies, although often rugged and austere, did not place the settler under an ever-threatening economic sword of Damocles. Turning to more elemental living in the wilderness today can, I think, alter advantageously the modern individual's present plight concerning economic security. It may be available, of course, only to those who can grasp the significance of what by contrast we need to consider wilderness values—essentially a more natural outlook. What it particularly amounts to is an intelligent modification of needless luxuries—by change of environment, decreased dependency upon the overwhelming complexity of artifice that engulfs most people in a pressured, conventional flood of disturbing materialism and urban stress.

But assuming that life has to be carried on in the metropolitan turmoil for various reasons, affluence per se does not necessarily become the promise of security. Potential victims of earthquakes, hurricanes, floods, brush and building fires, and other such hazards might well have on hand a mobile camper, for example, or better yet for the emergency moment, a complete lightweight camp outfit and emergency food rations consolidated in a packsack, stored in a handy closet from which it could be snatched in an instant while making an escape to an outlying area, rather than depending altogether on federal, municipal, or Red Cross help. In the same vein, the individual or family with a simple cabin tucked away on some wilderness fringe or waterfront, with a food supply, has a greater chance for security under survival stress than any immediate alternative.

It might become necessary under prolonged economic stress to abandon even the pretentious or modest home, if it has to be sustained by a top-level or middle income that has been reduced or cut off. Of course, it has to be presumed that we will, when possible under the circumstances named, salvage whatever we leave behind in the emergencies; but then life should also be so planned that even without this salvage we can still maintain a tenable existence in a cabin on the fringe or in the wilderness, where much of what we have to pay for elsewhere is often free.

Until the beginning of this century, common employment in winter fell off so radically that unless many employees had winter grubstakes for security, they faced dire need. The first onslaught of winter weather posed the question of what happened to last summer's wages. The solution was relatively simple for the wilderness-oriented individual. When the snow began to fly, he was soon comfortably ensconced in the fringe or in-depth wilderness cabin, his whole winter's food supply stored, and six months of leisurely living and time available for cultural improvement lying ahead. The world outside could virtually be tumbling down over the heads of many others, while he luxuriated in a measure of economic security.

We need not, of course, jump to the conclusion here that anyone can readily abandon the urban life he is living and seek the elemental pleasures and advantages of a wilderness life without considerable preparation. Too sudden a transition of life-style might prove, if not disastrous, then possibly a hapless floundering out of accustomed environment. What is needed is a systematic approach toward wilderness which can culminate in reality.

I know a man, for example, who though tied down to a job, got continued satisfaction from the early acquisition of a small tract of land fronting on a wild river, not too far from a tiny wilderness settlement. He avowed that some day he would build a cozy cabin and enjoy the leisure derived from his lifetime savings. It was enough in pleasant anticipation, planning, and learning to sustain him through those long years of employment which he said he just tolerated. Besides, in the event his immediate economic security were threatened, he felt he had a comforting alternative in this earlier, though modified, carrying out of his original cabin-building and living plan.

To know that if just about everything falls to a low level in the industrial world, you have the possibility of living without a compelling adherence to it, should make each night of sleep a bit more sound, each moment of living a bit more serene.

Approaches to wilderness living in search of security are not the whole story. People in all economic pursuits and levels of income or affluence are seeking ways of finding life patterns in a natural environment. On some television panel talk shows, for example, one learns about the lives of celebrities. Some, after highly remunerative careers, go on to such occupational diversions as ranch life, generally raising a special breed of stock for its added prestige value. Whatever the diversion, their most manifest desire seems to be to have a hand in some outdoor pursuit.

If we always have to give a conventional reason for getting away from urban pressures and into the open, then I say by all means use whatever worthwhile instrumentality becomes available to attain the desired natural end. A self-styled "hunter" once told me that in his tramps out of doors during hunting season, he carried a firearm merely to appear proper in his togs and outdoor pursuits, never firing his gun, never killing anything. This may seem a bit absurd, but how many of us have not in one way or another played the sedulous ape to convention?

Perhaps the strangest aspect of this transition program from urban life to life on the fringe or in the wilderness is that contemplated by the very affluent. One outdoors enthusiast I know had a seven-bedroom, highly modern structure in a semi-wild area, which he referred to as his "camp." At first he surrounded himself with close friends, acquaintances, and domestic help.

The Wilderness Life

As time went on he found the need for more solitude, more serenity, until finally he sought a new site and a much smaller, less visitor-accommodating structure that justified the appellation "camp."

Turning after a long life in an urban environment to the wilderness fringe as a security measure at retirement, judging from many examples, needs some qualifying warning. The danger lies in making the transition too abruptly. It is idealistic and delightful, of course, to think about suddenly leaving the grind and having long-sought leisure. But few have made the abrupt change with enduring success. The caged bird when given its freedom in a wilderness environment most likely will perish. That same bird by a slow transitory process from cage to aviary, and eventually from aviary to a gradual adjustment in the wilds, is likely to thrive.

Urban demands on the purse are usually too depriving for the retired to meet if they depend primarily on pensions and social security payments. Removed at least a nominal distance from the incessant daily demands of the cash register, pensions and social security can, on the other hand, generally prove ample. Living at the edge of or in the wilderness, even just beyond outer suburbia, can make such income, when properly handled, take on the appearance of economic splendor. There, by circumstance alone, dollar value increases substantially.

Living in a cabin on the fringe of or in the wilderness, one periodically has to make an outlay of money for supplies, of course, but there is not that daily cash drain. I need not emphasize the frequency with which one reaches for one's wallet in the city, where, figuratively speaking, innumerable hands are also reaching for it from every side. At the fringe of the wilderness, it is just a plain case of not needing or finding important the numerous things that money provided in the city. This is not a matter of deprivation but of replacing those things pertinent to city life that cost money with natural ones that in most instances in or near the wilds are free, and often possess greater pleasure value.

The seaside or lakefront estate of any pretension is a costly retreat, generally available only to the affluent. On the other hand, the small, cozy cabin on the waterfront can with less pretension have the same environmental values, with the additional assests of not being a white elephant to support. When you have so much wealth that it taxes the imagination to know how best to exploit nature with it, human and natural values tend to preempt more consideration than pretentious spending. We might consider that the luxury of sitting in the shade of a tree on a balmy summer day and contemplating a glorious scene is more leisurely achieved by the very poor and the very rich, because when you are very poor, money and time are not equated factors; and when you have become very rich, you discover that money does not have the all-encompassing importance you originally attributed to it in the gold rush of middle age.

In middle age, vacations are kept intentionally short in duration, because then one is convinced that time sold for dollars is an extraordinarily good bargain. As the years press on, the bargain does not look quite as good. Past middle age, one begins to wonder if the battering of so much time for dollars did not make one a victim of a swindle. Logic can never resolve this issue, but age inevitably does. When, late in life, one sits under a tree and contemplates the glory of a natural scene, there are fewer besetting apprehensions that one is wasting time; lack of time, then, is grimly recognized as the greatest poverty; every moment gleaned for leisure is realized as a splendid, priceless investment. If only this could be perceived earlier, how much greater would be the value of life's time!

The boy who yearned for a jackknife and one day was given a handful of jackknife samples, by a hardware salesman who was a friend of the family, suffered the disturbance of a precious thing in his youthful life—a sense of fundamental value. One jackknife can be a very desirable and priceless treasure; a dozen knives, to the romantic play of a boy's mind, may suddenly become instruments of confusion and despair. The adult with too many toys suffers ennui, and may never again enjoy the feeling of possessing something priceless.

When Thoreau suggested that we live in such a manner as to allow doing our bookkeeping on a thumbnail, he was, of course, speaking figuratively but wisely. The multiple accumulation of things in our lives today can become the clutter of tomorrow. Artful moderation, I insist, wears the diamond more graciously than does opulence.

6

The Early Trip

NEAR THE EARLY PART of the century, mapping
of the wilderness regions still rested on hypothesis, where
many rivers of the North were well defined for a short distance
inland on a map and then trailed off as conjectural dotted lines.
Lakes of great size were said to lie far inland, yet were still
known only by Indian legend. If one sought to travel by
canoe on just those waterways that had been well mapped out,
one did not belong to that fraternity for whom the aspiration
to adventure brought restless sleep.

For the adventurous, the silent places haunted, beckoned, and
challenged. One was quite sure that several weeks of canoe
travel along uncharted rivers, over portages unmarked and
unknown, would bring one to what at first sight seemed to be
a mysterious freshwater sea with forested, rockbound shores—
the undisturbed habitat of wilderness life. Such lakes as Du-
bawnt, Wollaston, Southern Indian, Reindeer, Athabasca, Great

Slave—any single one could be traveled on for weeks without its shores ever being fully explored.

Exploration is a catchword that has inspired many to strive to be first to appear on a scene for the glory the venture might have. Perhaps, unrealized, exploration has been the real reason for embarking on wilderness journeys, rather than the purported one of recreational pleasure alone. The planning and the going, not only achievement of arrival, can in either instance be further high points of the venture.

Even before the actual planning, there is the conception. As an idea, it might flicker momentarily as a spark and seem to go out. But that incipient spark *can* have the tiny nucleus of fire. Mere trial conversations with others may cause it to break into flame. Generally, canoe travel is most speculated about toward late winter when the snow is deepest, the temperature coldest, the prospect of spring almost too remote to anticipate. An evening among a few friends may be a casual one, when good food and leisurely conversation before an open fireplace suggest nothing more than congeniality. Then, without apparent provocation, there may develop the inception of a wilderness journey.

And that is how it happened when one evening I mentioned to a small group of friends around a fireplace that the greatest builder of birchbark canoes I knew, an Indian at Mille Lacs in Minnesota, was scheduled to make a birchbark canoe for me, to be delivered in the spring. One of the group asked, "What are you going to do with a birchbark canoe?" Facetiously, somebody replied, "You put it in the water."

At that time, commercial canoes were primarily the cedar strip, varnished Peterboroughs, the pride of canoe voyageurs. But there was something so elementally intriguing about the birchbark canoe, my choice became inevitable. Before the evening passed, two of us were laying the foundation for a voyage into Canada's wilds. Like "the best laid schemes of mice and men," however, it was destined to go awry.

As late summer settled over the north country and the birchbark canoe had been tested in local waters for its maiden wilderness voyage, my prospective partner lost his voyageur spirit. Pretexts were labored and obvious, winning out over adventure—a characteristic lesson about potential canoe partners I was to learn more than once, and well, in the ensuing years. The call of the wild too often gets lost in the noisy din of industry, or is preempted by social or domestic relations—even, now and then, by fear of the unknown.

By this time I had already committed the custom-making of a sailcloth tent to the nearest tentmaker; had at inordinate expense procured eiderdown and fine ticking for a sleeping unit; had acquired the finest single-blade cruiser-type ax available, then knocked out the factory handle and replaced it with one of select-grain hickory stock, and had ground the blade to deep-cutting thinness and provided it with a brass-lined, leather sheath; had equipped a Winchester carbine with sling and peep sight; had added a light, long-barreled, small-bore target pistol for small game; had my celestial navigation equipment altered at considerable factory expense for fixing positions in poorly mapped regions. In short, the investments I had been making on my limited budget were so oriented to wilderness travel that an abrupt return to conventional life would have resulted in sheer bankruptcy.

To find the particular canoe partner who might qualify became an ever-increasing problem, looming larger as the search for him went on. Austerity got in the way of several individuals who might have had or developed the capability. When affluence paved the way for certain prospective partners, I did not have the same experience which has been attributed to the war draft, that "the best soldiers came from Park Avenue mansions." Money had too often replaced manual dexterity. Also, where money became no object, it was largely a case of fathers merely wanting their already adult sons to "have a wilderness experience." Most often it was to get them out of impending mischief, generally of the kind where the opposite sex seemed incompatible with the family's financial and social standing. I was not, however, looking for a ward.

The best prospects among the well-to-do were serious-minded university students, who, being too involved in learning a profession, could not get away from school. When one of these was willing to give up his college education for a term to accompany me, and his parents looked upon me as interrupting his career, I considered wisdom the better part of valor, and again turned elsewhere. Vacation periods for students come during the fly season in the North, which is the poorest time for a canoe trip. Thus, the autumn months, being the select canoe travel season, ruled out the student.

The worlds of education, business, and industry, occupied with their functions, left me to flounder as best I could in the role of a social maverick. It is not difficult to understand how we can so readily be caught up in the conventional aggregation, not willing to suffer a kind of individualistic isolation—a traveling alone on a lone trail when the whole social caravan moves away majestically on a paved road.

This seeking a suitable partner for wilderness voyages was not to be my youthful experience only. As life went on into the later years, it became apparent that adventure in a most general application is not for the aggregate but for the intrepid individual, whether it is a voyage into the unknown wilderness or research into some unknown sphere of endeavor. It is the position that the quarterback faces when his defensive pocket is broken and he must either fall on the ball or risk injury in running with it.

It has been said, and no doubt rightly, that one of our fears, and perhaps the greatest, is fear of the unknown, or fear of fear itself. While since early boyhood I had been associated with the lesser wilderness, had camped along the rivers, lakes, and streams within reasonable accessibility, the vast wilderness of Canada lay in the mystery of overwhelming intrigue—almost a kind of fright. The lure, fortunately, was greater than the fright. Some of us have a love for crisis—an impulse to experience the threatening storm. It is the fascination of continuing when there is still an opportunity for retreat.

When my birchbark canoe was in the baggage car, along with camp equipment, and I realized that some irresistible force had me heading north alone, it seemed more like a dream than a reality. The dream was somewhat comparable to that of the fellow who dreamed that he was a soldier under hazardous gunfire, only to be awakened suddenly by a noise and find that he *was* a soldier under fire.

The train raced along river valleys through the predominantly deciduous growth of lower latitudes, past farmlands and through villages, some settlements important enough for a stop. It was, of course, country familiar to me, land mellowed by long occupancy, where cattle grazed and the fall harvest of golden grain fields had already begun. I splurged, eating a full meal in the diner, at a price I then thought bordered on larceny, but which today would buy only a snack. The wide dining car windows gave a magnificent view of the country, a luxury I tried to prolong. When I dallied so long that I found myself alone in the dining car, I sensed some tart looks from the steward that suggested I depart, so to delay my exit, I arrogantly ordered another pot of coffee.

Farms were becoming fewer and smaller. The vegetation began to indicate latitudinal change. The dense deciduous growth interspersed with occasional fir trees was being reversed. Now the forests became a dense growth of spruce, balsam, and pine—the sparse deciduous growth being moose maple, popple, and mountain ash. The train slowed somewhat when the right-of-way went through enormous spruce and tamarack bogs, the unballasted rail bed affected by heaving from alternate frost and thawing. No longer were there farms, and while earlier en route there had been towns, now there were mere wilderness settlements or significant mileposts, where half of the population loitering around the flagstops were Indians. The Indian women wore multicolored calicos, some faded, some bright. The Indian mothers carried their babies in *tikinakuns* on their backs. The men were dressed mostly in what seemed to be white man's cast-off street clothes, although a few among them wore buckskin shirts. The majority wore Indian-tanned, moosehide moccasins of the wraparound type, some elaborately beaded. Ostentation has been one of the most enduring primordial traits, as manifest certainly in modern society as in the primitive.

Leisure seemed to be more the tempo at the wilderness stops than in the earlier agricultural areas, no particular reason being apparent for the longer delays in the wilderness area. At one of these stops several Indians peered into the baggage car with much interest and talk about the *wuskwicheman,* my birchbark canoe. When they learned from the baggage clerk that it did not belong to an Indian but to a white man, their curiosity was further aroused. One of the younger Indians, acting as translator, conveyed the information to me that his people thought it very fine workmanship and wanted to know if I had made it. When I told him that it was made by an older woodland Indian at Mille Lacs Lake in Minnesota, the translation had its greatest reference to *kisayinew* (an older Indian), but somehow the name Minnesota did not get translated. Then I realized that *Minnesota* is an Indian name, closer perhaps to the Sioux tongue, meaning "clouded or milky water," though possibly understood by the Cree.

A number of half-starved sled dogs of a mongrelized husky breed loitered about. When the time of cold weather would draw near, they would be more amply fed to make them strong for their winter task. I tossed the small remaining part of a candy bar to one of the dogs, which brought two others furiously rushing to the scene, almost precipitating a fight. They bared wolfish teeth and growled, then looked to me for further tidbits.

Presently, I heard a low-pitched "All Aboard." The train raced around the curves created by lakes, skirting them so closely at the water's edge as to give the impression to one looking through the train's lakeside windows of being aboard a watercraft.

In an area that seemed to offer no possible reason for a stop, the train came to a screeching-of-brakes slowdown and then ran slowly for about a half mile. As the train began picking up speed again, I saw two moose lumbering off the railroad right-of-way into the forest at no apparently urgent gait. The conductor explained that the moose had been running down the track ahead of the train. Soon I would be leaving the train at a tiny Ontario settlement, if a milepost could be called that. The moose suggested the kind of country into which I would shortly be pointing the bow of my birchbark canoe northward.

The railroad had been built through that area only by

horse-drawn scraper and black powder blasting. The country itself that early still lay as wild as it had been millennially. To the southwest about two hundred miles was Lake Superior and the immensity of its basin, its waters heading into the Gulf of the St. Lawrence and the Atlantic, eventually washing Newfoundland's shores. But here at my feet was a river on a different watershed, running through a spectacular wilderness of forest and bedrock, the Precambrian shield, to Lake Winnipeg, the lake water moving indiscernibly yet flowing three hundred miles more to the north of the lake, where the waters spill into the Nelson River to wind through hundreds of miles of rockbound shore to Hudson Bay, mixing into a compound of fresh and salt water through Hudson Straight with the waters of the North Atlantic Ocean.

Had I planned this jumping-off place to the wilderness more selectively, I could not have aspired to a greater center for departure on canoe trips. According to the map, I stood at the hub of a geographical wheel, the waterway spokes to the interior wilderness tantalizingly varied in their allure.

A dozen or more Indians were at the rail stop. More hands than were needed lifted the birchbark canoe and my two Poirer packs from the baggage car. And here again, the construction of the birchbark caught the Indians' fancy. They handed the canoe gently, almost it seemed reverently, turning it over to examine every detail. They remarked about the bottom being of one piece, which I learned is an earmark of good birchbark canoe construction. The canoe had been built far enough from their own area evidently for them to notice a difference, though slight, in the material and workmanship used in the construction. The women commented about the excellent work done in the sewing and gumming of the *wattap* seams—a task traditionally theirs. They, too, wanted to know if I had made the canoe. "No," I said, "Eyinew" (Indian), which seemed to please them. The birchbark canoe was, after all, not truly the white man's province, although white men in the fur trade had surely become involved with its construction, some of the big thirty-five-foot Montreal canoes having been used in travel from the coast to the Grand Portage. I had been made fully aware that all of the materials for repair of a birchbark canoe could be had in the wilderness area where I now would travel.

After the train departed, the Indians and the few whites among them vanished quickly; I found myself wondering about my next move. I learned that the Indians were camped across the river where it came out of an expansive lake area, the lake being a widening of the river, a situation that is repeated on the river chains of the vast canoe country to the north.

Portaging my two packs, one of equipment and the other provisions, and the canoe to the waterfront in two trips, I paddled a short distance up the shore, and found a small area for a camp. Across the water, I could see smoke rising from the Indian campfires, and shortly sent up a smoke streamer of my own. I hoped that it might impart a smoke signal gesture of good will, perhaps prompt a visit from one or two of their party, but night fell without any arrivals. Indians have a remarkable ability for minding their own affairs.

Little more than a sliver of a moon was visible above the forest, slipping in and out of rain clouds. As darkness deepened, the Indian campfires loomed clearer. Silhouetted figures moved about now and then between me and the flames. I wondered what conclusion they had drawn about my presence in the region. Without the birchbark canoe as a possible bond between us, I might have been given only the meager notice afforded a tourist. Perhaps the addition of the Indian-tanned, Indian-

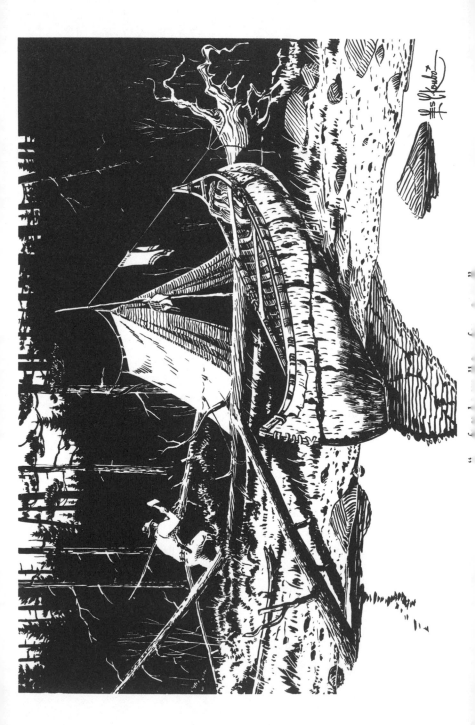

fabricated buckskin shirt I wore further complemented the possible bond. But no mention had been made of it at the rail stop. Indian decorum might sanction interest in so impersonal an item as the construction of a birchbark canoe, but for them to comment on one's clothes might be only the prerogative of people very close to the wearer. One of the Indians at the station wore a calf moosehide shirt, and unless vanity proves to belie my observations, I thought the Indian women were stealing a few fleeting side-glances at the style and workmanship of my own Indian-made shirt.

The cost of an Indian guide in those early days would seem a mere pittance today, but the pittance of today was the extravagance of yesterday. I needed a companion, although I was in no financial position to hire one in the role of a guide. What I hoped for was an Indian companion.

Without really having the empirical qualification at the time for thinking so, I did presume it to be somewhat of a weakness not to be able to cope with life in the wilds without a guide. This, in any case, can be a wrong concept. Good guides can teach not only the inexperienced—the exchange of ideas between two experienced woodsmen can be a knowledge-enrichment for both. Above all, as an aspirant I was amenable and anxious to learn something of Indian methods and life.

When my own campfire had died down, and I was ready to sack in for the night, the Indian campfires also had become only glowing embers. My own fire felt good. Even in August the northern night often has enough chill for one to enjoy the folds of a sleeping robe or the warmth of a fire.

On awakening the next morning, I found that rain was pattering on my tent. I raised one side for a canopy and started a small breakfast fire beneath it. Skies were leaden, and the surrounding forest was dripping. A fog hung over the water, so dense that I could not fully determine if there was smoke rising from the Indian camp until I went to the rockbound shore for water to make coffee. The barely perceptible odor of a fresh fire, not my own, drifted in across the water.

Regardless of whether I could acquire a companion among the Indians, I decided to stay in camp and wait out the rain before starting out alone. Inevitably, one experiences rain sooner or later on a canoe journey; but somehow, for the sake of one's initial outlook, the start, if not too delayed, must get under way in clear weather.

After breakfast I threw a canoe tracking line over the limb of a tree and hoisted the heavy food pack well above the ground to prevent it becoming a rainy-day feast for bears; then, leaving the tent pitched and wide open to prevent bears tearing their way into it for inspection, I set out in the birchbark canoe across the short span of water for the Indian camp.

Their chief and two much younger males came to the waterfront. Disregarding the drizzle and without rain gear, they welcomed me ashore. I was clad in a pullover rain shirt, rain hat, and lightweight, four-buckle overshoes. As they helpfully lifted my canoe on shore, one of the younger men examined my canoe paddle, an Algonquin shape, where the blade is broader near the shaft than at the end. The common canoe paddle used by most Indians in those days was generally custom-hewn out of the wood cut in the immediate forest, a rather short paddle. This accounts for the short, though very effective, rapid stroke of the Indian's paddling. The commercially made Algonquin paddle I had was almost a foot longer, which is universally quite standard today.

Just how I would be accepted in the camp I did not know until the moment I was met at the shore by the three Indians. Then all apprehensions faded. They were very cordial. My inquiries about the upper country were answered in detail. The young crowded around but said nothing. The women held themselves aloof in the background, though curious.

I had a plan. I would buy a supply of provisions and throw a kind of potlatch, inviting all of the Indians. This would surely, I figured, be within my means. I could then talk casually about a possible companion, having an advantage under the circumstances of studying whoever might be a potential partner for the trip, if indeed one of them should desire to go along.

I did not tarry too long on my visit. I knew that my best approach was to give the impression that the potlatch idea had been a spontaneous one. I was served tea and moosemeat before leaving, though I still had a breakfast under my belt. It was an ideal moment to suggest that they pay me a return visit at my camp, which a few promptly agreed to do; but when I said that all should come, a moment of hilarity broke out among the women. With eighteen people in the camp, it seemed to them that I had bitten off more than a mouthful of feasting.

Just what I would serve to eighteen healthy Indians and myself without knowing what they liked, and what was on hand at the trading post, became a puzzle until I talked to the trading post manager, who had dealt with Indians for a long time.

"Hell," he said, "make it easy for yourself. Give them canned beans, wieners, and a hell of a lot of bread and butter. They like butter."

I borrowed two large pots from the Indians, one for the beans, the other for the wieners. Before I could get under way, the chief said that two of the women would prepare the food and bring the eating utensils, while two of them would come over to my camp spot to "brush out," or clear, a little more space. What seemed considerate here was that no suggestion was made to have the potlatch in the Indian camp where there was plenty of cleared space. I had invited them to my camp and decorum told them that the invitation must be respected.

Not a word was mentioned about the rain, which now, though holding off for the time being, promised no immediate relief. About an hour after noon a few blue holes appeared in the cloudy sky, and when late in the afternoon the flotilla of Indians came across the river in their canoes, not a cloud was visible. I must have a good standing with the *Kiche Munito* (Great Spirit), they commented, to have the skies clear when I wanted them to.

The chief seemed well the master of his position, for it took but a few quietly uttered Cree words to direct whatever was needed, though I also sensed a strong matriarchal presence when the two women who were occupied with preparing the food gave their orders. If caterers in the conventional world seem to be competent in organizing party food, they could not have done better than those two Indian women who prepared and served a banquet of beans and wieners. I suggested that we raise our tin tea cups and drink a toast to the chief, the two cooks, and the two men who had cleared the brush for the needed space. My "Hip, Hip, Hurrah!" may not have been fully recognized as a tribute, but they all went along with it in a gay and understanding mood, laughter becoming quite spontaneous.

The Indian lives with a leisure and an empathy for his fellow man that is magnificent. I wanted a companion, and the naturalness with which this came about seemed intuitively grasped.

The two Indians who had cleared the area for the potlatch intimated that if I wanted a companion on my trip, either one of them was willing to go along. They determined between themselves who it would be. Since the older of the two spoke only a few words of English, he deferred to the younger, who much earlier had been off to a mission school for a year. Our fairly equal youthful age might also have entered into the choice.

Perhaps it was my rather sophisticated camp equipment that seemed to promise my companion, Osimisk, which was shortened to Ossy, a good journey, for he and the chief spoke highly of every item, from my tent on down. I had brought along an extra rain shirt and hat, knowing from experience that few people have wholly proper wilderness rain gear. But, somehow, that rain gear did not get donned except when there was prolonged heavy rain. A small wetting to the Indian was less of a nuisance than the continual donning and shedding of gear, and I myself came to adopt this plan after a time. A rabbit-skin sleeping robe, a sheath knife, and a few items of clothing were all that Osimisk added to our general equipment. The chief was intrigued by my sextant and artificial horizon.

When I expressed a desire to get under way on our canoe journey, the chief and Osimisk's brush-cutting partner paddled a second canoe with us seven miles to the upper part of the lake, where we stopped on an island to observe the roughness of the water beyond—an uninterrupted, widened stretch of the river about five miles across. The waves were high and torn at the top by whitecaps. The chief, seeing what he called the *mukahun* (big waves), suggested that we camp on the island and cross the five miles of water to the portage trail well into the night when the lake usually settles down to a calm. Years later, on successive canoe trips when traversing big water, I followed this procedure. It is part of the edification, the many experiences one gathers in traveling with Indians and others long associated with the wilds.

The Wilderness Life

The chief and his companion stayed with Osimisk and me until we took off shortly after midnight. A heavy overcast having built up, we used a compass course to make the night crossing, landing on a sandy beach within a very short error-distance from the actual portage. While we were paddling across the semi-calm water, I asked Osimisk what his name meant, since Indian names are so descriptively colorful. He said that it meant bud, an appellation which I immediately construed to be a shortening of buddy. Then he told me that translated, it meant a bud or leaflet.

"Shall I call you Ossy or Bud?" I asked. He chose Bud, so Bud it was through almost two months of travel in Ontario's and Manitoba's magnificent canoe country, to discover with one of its own the miracle which is wilderness.

A week of travel, camping, and revelations of the wild had passed before Bud and I had made the adjustment to each other in which I would be able to observe the innate qualities of the long-habituated Indian. Perhaps because I had initiated the trip and invited him as a partner, he felt the need to respect my efforts too much, deferring to whatever I seemed destined at the moment to do. I wanted to see the true, uninhibited native long-assimilated to his environment.

One night as we sat around a campfire, Bud not saying very much, I made a speech that must have pleased him. The gist of it was that his ancestors had lived and traveled for centuries in the very wilderness where we now were, that they had become a part of it and had made him a part of it.

"I have to learn in a short time," I said, "what comes natural to you, an Indian. Starting tomorrow morning, will you be the teacher so that I can get to be more a part of the wilderness, and be more like an Indian?"

The ring of sincerity in my voice, perhaps, had more effect

than what I had said. The following morning Bud was out of bed ahead of me, whereas in the preceding days he waited until I rolled out of my sleeping bag. I thought about people in the city whom I had visited overnight, where I dared not arise until I heard a stirring in the house. The pack of store provisions was scarcely touched under Bud's cooking tutelage, although some of the items tickled his palate. We now began living off the country. The fishnet was in the water more frequently. At times, Bud would be gone for hours and return with various game birds or other meat. Only the two largest of four nested cooking pails were used by him, whereas I invariably had every utensil in operation at the meals I cooked. Bud made tea in one, and as for the other, we always had a one-dish meal.

I watched him on the portage trails, as a cub reporter might watch a news bit in which he had to report every detail. Bud's stride, the swing of his body, his way of weaving the canoe through brush-filled portage trails, always seemed to be accomplished, if not with a minimum of effort, then certainly without any apparent effect of a struggle. Part of the secret was that to him, brushy trails, heavy seas, protracted rough weather, and other obstacles to complacency were taken as a matter of course, not regarded as unfortunate circumstances. How basically important, I thought many times as we traveled together, was this attitude, which could be considered as a philosophy of life anywhere.

One might be tempted here to go from the early rise in the morning to every simple function of an Indian's day. For want of space, I might rather encompass his hour-to-hour moves in the single term "facility." Our fishnet, weighted along the lower edge and floating on top—the mode of handling fishnets —he cast into the riffles below the falls, tethering it to a shore mooring with a single dexterous move or two, whereas I would be inclined to fuss with it. When we reached a portage trail, the packs went from the canoe to his back and over the trail with a succession of rhythmic movements, rather than from the canoe to a possible dry spot on the ground during subsequent reflection on who should carry what. I built cooking fires with methods of campcraft propriety, only to find that Bud's kettle was boiling almost in the time I had assembled tinder and a supply of wood. Often he would stop along a portage trail in spite of a heavy load on his back, to pick up just what fuel he wanted in order to have a fire going quickly for tea at the other end of the portage.

It became obvious that some of the items, which I presumed to have practical value, and that I had carried on my pack over miles of portage trails, were wholly extraneous to Bud and the facile trail life of the Indian. I had paid dearly for them with my low budget; yet, without a word of comment from Bud, I left them hanging in trees beside trails—gadgets that *when abandoned* gave added facility to wilderness life.

Strangely, Bud gave no notice of them hanging in the trees, nor did he make any remarks about the expedience gained without them. Obviously, there was a lesson here in human relations.

As the weeks went by, what I saw in the Indian's mode of living and meeting the wilderness on its own terms was his way of staying bracketed in between no facility other than that offered by the wilds, and white man's encumbering gadgetry. Just where the demarcation line should be drawn between needed facilities and those which encumber movement is a problem in most wilderness travel, if not in life generally. Most of us err on the side of needless encumbrance, whether we are in the city or wilderness. Using more than we need is to rob ourselves of the time to acquire it and to handicap ourselves after we have it to protect and hope to use it. What I found in associating with the Indian and Eskimo under natural conditions is that they have generally learned the lesson about encumbrance that we in conventional society fail to learn. They have the faculty of deleting for convenience, whereas we have the malady of accumulating until we are distressed with the load.

Late one afternoon toward the end of the seventh week of wilderness travel, we paddled down the last stretch of water to Bud's Indian home camp. About half of the families had left for their trapping grounds in the interior; the others were making ready for departure. But we were met on the waterfront with a memorable welcome by those who remained.

I left my canoe, tent, and guns with Bud, who had lived with them long enough to have full equity. The canoe he and I had patched a number of times, and no doubt he would patch it again and again. Years later when I returned to the Indian camp, Bud had gone elsewhere and I was not to see him again. But I had a cue-in, as it were, with the Indians as a result of Bud's and my trip together; and as indicated in another narrative herein, what I had learned from Bud was to be tested by his successors.

7

In Search of Fulfillment

A SHORT TIME AGO, I arrived in a great metropolis en route from the wilds. The city's population moved like a stream in flood along its walks, while cars inched by almost bumper to bumper. A week or so earlier, I had looked out over a vast wonderland of sunlit, rockbound lakes and coniferous forests, without seeing a human being—a disproportion of habitat that evoked strange thought. Breathing the fresh air of the wilds for several months, my throat now unaccustomed to the city was sensitive to the effluent of smoking chimneys and car exhaust. I reasoned that many of the people milling by me had to be where they were by circumstances beyond their immediate control. Then, on second thought, I had to presume that many of them surely had the option and means to be wherever they wished. If so, why did they choose to be where they were?

I suppose it is true that the way to have empathy with anyone is, as the saying goes, to walk in his shoes for a while. And since this is not possible, we can never hope to discover what the thousands who mill by on the sidewalk seek as fulfillment. The saying, "One can write the biography of most people forty years in advance, barring accidents," recklessly omits numerous people who may have found individualistic and durable life-styles for themselves and for others, but could not, for reasons beyond their control, realize them.

When one canvasses the public for answers as to what they seek as life's fulfillment, a composite answer is often best expressed by a pearl of wisdom that falls not from the mouth of a sage but from that of an ordinary citizen. One of these said, "People don't know what the hell they want."

We are told by psychologists that the majority of people are "floundering to some extent outside their environment; and if not floundering, then at least wriggling uncomfortably." Perhaps most of us would agree to the latter, if only we could fully conceive what that environment might be. It became obvious to me rather early in life that I would be compelled to flounder, or at least wriggle uncomfortably, in the urban environment periodically for a certain length of time each year, in order to earn the means to abide in the environment of my choice, which narrowed down to somewhere in the millions of square miles of the United States' and Canada's vast wilderness.

In spite of this aversion, I did manage to find an urban occupation in which I wriggled minimally by virtue of its intrinsic adventure. I became an investigator of crime, and succeeded well enough in running down incorrigibles, riding through seven years of the worst period of gangsterism in the country's history.

A day came when even this palled. Perhaps momentous

decisions, like high dives, are best achieved by sudden impulse rather than deliberation. I abruptly quit what I was doing and took up life in a cabin on one of the forested, rockbound streams that tumble into Lake Superior's basin.

There were, of course, the usual inducements to return to work periodically. This was especially true when the scene of criminal or civil investigation shifted to some remote wilderness area. Most investigators on our staff professed to be more the products of the city than I. When a case required the combining of forces with some sheriff or member of the provincial or Royal Canadian Mounted Police, well beyond the pale of the city, my own specialization came into play. Also, there was the eternal need to return to work in order to earn my subsistence from time to time.

That much labored cliché that if you build a better mousetrap, the world will beat a path to your door, has after all, I am convinced, a grain of truth in it. One morning as I relaxed in my cabin, eating breakfast, concerned with little more than the chattering of a friendly red squirrel that appeared regularly outside my door, I heard a knock. The visitor was a Canadian barrister—a stranger to me—accompanied by a local Indian guide whom I knew very well.

Whatever the grapevine of communication, the barrister advised me that I had been recommended to him through a New York office as one who might be able to find, somewhere in Canada's wilderness, a member of a British family who had become heir apparent to a substantial sum of money. What proved about as apparent as his being the heir was that he would not be likely to be found in a city. General information about him left some question as to whether he would even be found on the North American continent. That his interest was centered in natural environments offered a clue, but a vague one. He had spent considerable time in the wilderness areas of New Zealand, South Africa, and a short period in Spitsbergen, those subarctic islands north of the Scandinavian peninsula; but he had finally shown a strong affinity for the wilds of Canada, which he had visited over the years on several occasions for extensive periods. He would, he had told his own people, "settle some day on a Canadian wilderness waterfront."

How simple! All I had to do was find the waterfront. Ontario alone has about one hundred thousand lakes. Also, there was no certainty that he had settled. Peripatetic as he was, he might still be searching not only for the ideal waterfront but, vaguely, for some fulfillment of life, which could be about as elusive to him as his whereabouts might prove to us.

Having spent considerable time in my cabin on Lake Superior's basin since leaving my job, I was no less interested in a bit of vagabonding myself.

It became apparent that there would be more to an effort to fulfill the task assigned to me by the barrister than just finding a stick and proceeding to beat the thousands of square miles of Canada's bush.

The barrister did, encouragingly enough, provide me with a duplicate file to study. It had copies of the subject's letters from various parts of the world, including Canada, which at least showed a general geographical interest. As some of the dates of the Canadian letters were found to be more recent, so also did the letters become fewer, and the postmarks more widely scattered. Checks from England had cleared through Canadian banks, but these, too, were from diverse locations.

Time was of the essence, though not of such urgency, I was told, as to prevent weeks or even months of search, if necessary. It was obvious that in order to eliminate many of the clues I had in the file as to the possible whereabouts of the subject, I would need to anchor myself regionally in various places where I could combine Canada's telephone system with the wilderness grapevine.

In a small village on the Gypsomville Railroad between Lake Winnipegosis and Lake Winnipeg, I went to a local, residential, telephone exchange to make a call. When I had far exceeded the average time for a cross-Canada long distance call, the operator became panicky, cut in, and reminded me at intervals of the mounting bill. In her anxiety, she called in a local businessman, who waited unperturbed until I was through, then gave me the phone tab, commenting as I paid him, "The phone company will be your eternal friend."

At times it became difficult to make financial arrangements for someone in tiny hamlets and mileposts to check out various bits of information, although some of the phone operators and supervisors demonstrated marked ingenuity. After my week of generously patronizing the telephone company, I had completed the spade work which now would require my more direct, on-the-ground effort. A few possibilities hung in the balance, none very encouraging. It seems that the heir apparent had been as interested in seeing the various regions of Canada for their scenic grandeur and special attractions as he was in finding that ideal cabin site on a waterfront. While he had been in the places where I managed contact and had seemingly been comfortably ensconced in rented cabins for a fair amount of time, the answer I got was always disappointingly the same: "He's not here now."

After sixty years of living off and on in Canada's wilderness areas and its settlements, I am still not sure whether the Canadian conventional telephone and the radio telephone, or the so-called grapevine, is the most efficient communication system, although all of them in complement tend to amaze at times. Whenever I moved, I left a forwarding address for telephone operators to find me, even though I was only to board a certain train.

One day as I sat in a dining car on the coast-to-coast train, enjoying the pleasure of dining with several interesting Canadian citizens, I was handed a telegram that had apparently been attached to one of those rattan hoops which trainmen snatch on the fly from signal posts. The message was from a private citizen in a small settlement which I had telephoned because of a postmark to check the possible presence of the subject in that place. In the various instances I had told the operator that I would talk to anyone who would listen.

The telegram read, "Indians here say maybe your man. I think they right."

The grammatical construction of the message was interesting. The "maybe" I pondered, but the "I think they right," added enough assurance to compel my personal investigation.

As circumstances had it, my train was headed the wrong way to reach the settlement, which necessitated a transfer at the next scheduled stop. I had given the conductor an answer to the telegram, which he promised to dispatch somewhere ahead.

The local train pulled into the tiny forest settlement late at night. When its thundering sound left silence in its wake, I heard muffled voices coming from the river, and soon the sound of a canoe being beached. Before I reached the river from where the sounds came, I met two Indians who told me that they were camped a short distance away on the river bank, waiting for me to arrive.

The dialogue that followed was classically brief. "Do you know the man I'm looking for?" I asked.

"Sure. He marry my sister," one of them replied.

The Wilderness Life

When he told me that his brother-in-law did not have the same name as the man I was looking for, the dark, magnificent river, lit by a thin sliver of a moon and countless stars, lost some of its nocturnal grandeur.

In my Poirer pack I had a light, high-count poplin tent, a down sleeping robe, some cooking utensils, and about a two-day ration of food. I was now tempted to give the Indians some sort of honorarium for their efforts, dismiss them, and on the first piece of ground I could find, pitch a tent until train time, convinced that I had been led on another wild goose chase. But as a matter of thorough routine practice I had to check out a factor or two before I could totally dismiss the possible lead.

By now we had reached the canoe landing. Out of my pack I produced a flashlight and from my file two photos of the subject which had been taken quite a few years earlier. The two Indians crowded in closer to observe them, seemed a bit excited, but had indecision in their every word and action, exchanging remarks in Cree, as though in argument. The discourse was that the brother-in-law had a beard, was older, perhaps fifty, yet looked like the picture.

We went on to their camp on the river and rekindled a fire, while I prepared some food. The Indians talked vociferously to each other, again examining the picture by the light of the flames, and finally said, "That him."

As we ate, I asked further qualifying questions. Would anyone else in the tiny settlement be able to identify him? How tall was he? What color were his eyes? His hair? Much was encouraging in their replies, but nothing seemed conclusive.

The following day my inquiries and the submitting of photos to various people made identification fairly certain. The beard did not prove too disguising. Also, I had gathered other identifying material relating to the subject's history which left only one question. What about the change in name? Was he trying to live incognito? Could there be some question as to his integrity? The police I had phoned had no counts against him. He seemed to be of good character and intelligent.

While he did get his mail and provisions at the railroad settlement trading post, in most instances these were picked up by the Indians, the subject making an appearance only a time or two each year from a cabin deep in the wilderness, and then always accompanied by his wife.

From a private residence where I had obtained a room, I called the barrister, as I had done periodically. It seemed he was expecting just one more report in the slow process of elimination. When I told him that I believed I had learned of the subject's whereabouts deep in the wilds but was troubled about the identity since the name did not fit, it proved to be the clinching factor in making identification conclusive. The subject was an adopted son. While there had been no apparent unpleasant estrangement between him and his foster parents, he had at some point evidently decided to take the name of his blood parents.

The barrister asked if I could make the canoe journey of about one hundred miles to the interior wilderness, and explain the circumstance of the inheritance to the subject. Besides the two Indians and their canoe, I now needed a second canoe and another Indian as a paddler, along with provisions for the trip. The route was to be over a course of rivers and portages. I tried to rent a canoe but found only a newly purchased one available, which the owner was willing to part with at a price. When I explained this to the barrister, his answer brought a quick solution.

"Buy it, whatever it costs," he said, "and anything else you need. Put it on your expense account. Just keep the canoe and whatever else you require."

Money isn't everything, but it certainly smooths a rough course at times.

I was now virtually in the position of having three guides. The Indians insisted upon carrying everything over the portages, pitching the camps and cooking. When the rapids seemed rough and I suggested that we portage around the worst ones, they ran the canoes as single paddlers through them, performing spectacular whitewater feats.

In a few days the new canoe was beginning to look assimilated to trail use. While it had not actually been abused, it showed the usual paint scrapes acquired in some of the shallower, boulder-strewn rapids. One of the Indians had been in military service and referred to the scrapes as "service stripes." All three Indians were good canoe men, although in their eagerness to prove it to me, and being young enough to welcome adventure, competitiveness made them more reckless than was good for the canoe paint and even at times, I thought, for their own safety. I had, as usual, packed my equipment and provisions in waterproof packs that would float. One cascade, on which I would not allow my canoe to be run, one of the Indians in bravado attempted with his own canoe. Ten minutes later at the lower end of the portage we fished out a swamped canoe, some floating but half-submerged packs, and a very embarrassed, slightly disgruntled, and bruised Indian from the river below the rapids. With the American Indian, as with everybody, there is a strong desire for competition. The upset did have the value of tempering this overplayed competition during the balance of the trip.

Nevertheless, high spirits prevailed among us, whether on the portages or in camp. When the rains came too heavily, I suggested that we remain dry in camp, although the Indians, Spartan-like, were willing to travel. On the sixth day, about two hours after daylight, we portaged over a series of falls to a lake, where the Indians pointed out log cabin buildings on the far shore. The peeled, varnished logs shone like gold in the morning sunlight. This struck me as sort of symbolic, although I kept the idea to myself. We might have continued, but we would then have arrived awkwardly after dark and created an inconvenience, even though I was told that a spare cabin was available.

Two canoes and four paddles flashing on the sunlit lake the following morning were not apt to escape detection. On our arrival, the subject of my search stood on the rocky shore where I was deposited by the Indians, while they swung off into a sandy shore bay and beached the canoes. From the porch of the largest cabin, a fine-figured woman, perhaps in her middle thirties, came to the water's edge. Her complexion, somewhat lighter than that of the Indian who had remarked, "He marry my sister," showed some lineage of both white and Indian ancestry. Her deference to the subject's conversation with me gave her a manner that might best be described by the word "polished."

If I had expected to find a sourdough-type subject and his wife living a rugged life in the backwoods, the expectation would have been far removed from reality. What I had learned from the Indians while on the canoe route refuted any such notion. Neither was he a remittance man, one of those individuals who for some reason or other could not fit into England's society and was dispatched to Canada or to some other commonwealth country with an annual remittance, to keep him from being a thorn in the formal family's social side. He impressed me as a man of education and intellectual stature.

"Two canoes were not apt to avoid detection."

I was at a loss to know just how to approach him with the information of his inheritance. I thought he might be grief-stricken on learning about certain deaths that had provided the windfall. When I remarked that I had some business I would like to discuss with him, his wife made a graceful overture toward leaving the subject alone with me. "We have no secrets," he said, and insisted his wife remain while I outlined what I had to convey from the file I carried. This, of course, was brief. The barrister had instructed me only to find the subject, convey the inheritance circumstance, and arrange a meeting at some point on the railroad where the matter would be concluded. I reported the deaths, news which the subject received in silence. That he was an important heir to what I presumed to be a considerable amount of money did not visibly seem to affect him.

The three Indians who had accompanied me on the trail had disappeared—where to, I did not know. They reappeared when we had lunch. All of us sat at a table of unique design, excellently handcrafted from planed, knotty pine boards, and varnished. We ate from dishes of English china set on colorful linen—a surprising decor, I thought, this far back in the wilds.

Little had been said by the three Indians until they were asked about our canoe trip from the railroad. Then there was some subdued laughter when two of them told about the third having swamped in the rapids. Each of us in turn contributed some anecdote of our own in which we had at one time or another made a trail blunder, thus dispelling any further embarrassment suffered by the Indian who had swamped.

The subject's marriage to an Indian girl had obviously given him great rapport with the Indians in the district, through which he had their valuable help as log cabin builders and the means of getting supplies by canoe from the railroad. Apparently, among the Indians in the immediate area were some excellent builders, for the workmanship of the log cabin was unusually good. The building site had been well chosen, offering ample flat ground above the high water mark for the needed buildings: the main cabin of three rooms, auxiliary cabins, a combination storage and workshop, a meat cache, and a ramada-like structure for drying and storing wood.

My guided tour of the place was inspiring. The neatness, the competent choice of wilderness equipment, the view in three advantageous directions through island-dotted water, and the manner of those who were directly and indirectly associated with the premises, formed a grand impression and elicited a compound of feeling about the place that has remained with me and has influenced much of what I have done in respect to building craft and wilderness living in subsequent years.

The question that kept running through my mind was: if the subject had in a sense dissociated himself from his affluent family in England, how was he able, without apparent employment, to maintain the status in which he lived? What did he do for an income? Obviously, he had paid generously to have things built. This matter of income was, of course, too delicate a topic for me to broach. Part of the answer came voluntarily when in casual conversation we walked out on a rocky promontory with an impressive view, to find a place windy enough to keep away whatever insects might bother us.

"Some small trees wound their gnarled roots around this high rock formation when I first came here," he said, "but I removed the trees to get full play of the wind." The various rock elevations made a dozen good places to sit.

"I am amazed," I said, "at what you have here; and naturally, I am curious as to how it came about." I did not think this was too provocative.

He avoided it by asking, "How did you find me?" Then before I could answer, he added somewhat wryly, "I wasn't hiding."

He went on to explain that he was living a life neither of a recluse nor of a remittance man, nor in conflict with society. He and his wife spent a part of the year in cities—in Montreal, Winnipeg, and Vancouver. As time ran on, he explained, they were spending more of each year here in the seclusion of their wilderness home.

He had left England with ample means, he told me, explaining that his investments in Canada would suffice to keep the household economy in good shape for the rest of their lives. "The inheritance, however, will be welcome," he concluded, "since it will offer an opportunity to help some of the people around here."

I interrupted long enough to ask what he meant by, "around here." He smiled, made a sweeping gesture and said, "My nearby neighbors within a hundred miles or so."

I was persuaded to stay on at least until he had to make the trip out to meet the barrister in some city on the railroad. Impulsiveness, obviously, was not his nature. He would have two of the Indians make a trip to the railroad and contact the barrister by phone for an appointment. The Indians, I knew, would travel faster if I were not on the trip. Once this rendezvous was established, he and his wife, one of the Indians, and I could proceed to the railroad in two canoes. His general nonchalance and deliberate manner about the whole matter left me with an enduring calm.

This nonchalance was not, of course, what first I expected, although the general tempo of his living was what I would also have chosen for my own. The common current stress pattern of conventional life suggested to me that he would be quite over-

whelmed with the news of receiving a large sum through
inheritance, and would move with the greatest dispatch to
meet the barrister and acquire the proceeds of his good fortune.
But his mode of living apparently had tempered acquisitiveness,
if it had in fact ever been part of his nature.

The following morning I watched two of the Indians who
had accompanied me from the railhead pack food and equipment for the trip to arrange the meeting with the barrister. I
caught the contagious high spirits involved in their travel to
the railroad. While there was no apparent excitement about
their preparations, one sensed evidence of suppressed joy in the
prospect of their making the journey. It was my impression
from what the Indians had said that they were paid a per diem
wage only when they made these trips and when they worked
around the camp.

Once the Indians' canoe was out of sight, the subject, his
wife, the remaining Indian, and I settled down to a more
tranquil life. What became of special interest to me was
essentially the character of an individual who, having the
advantage of wealth and education, chose to spend most of
his life in the wilderness. I was hoping in some way to correlate
my own general attitude with his. To crowd this curiosity on
my part called for more diplomacy and decorum than I felt I
possessed. Should I be straightforward in my questions and
assume that he would be forthright in his answers? On the
other hand, any effort toward circuity would be readily discovered by such an intelligent individual, and would perhaps
carry the implication that his choice of life-style might be in
question.

With my purview, of course, it never would be. Where I
lived on the river that spilled into Lake Superior, I was among
whites, Indians, and persons of mixed ancestry. Ethnically, I

leaned heavily toward the rather placid life-style of the American Indian, perhaps being even a bit envious of his traditional ease of adjustment to the wilderness.

One evening as we sat relaxed in the main cabin before the open fireplace, I felt that both the subject and his wife had sensed what I secretly pondered. Mentioning his wife by her first name, he said, "If I hadn't met her in Montreal, seen her adjust to the metropolis and as well to the wilderness trips we took, I might still be wandering around the world, or at least roaming through Canada, in search of some possible elusive fulfillment of life. She has been my answer to everything. We are happy here."

I had hoped for some comment from her, but if anyone can draw conclusions from pantomime, I saw only delightful agreement. She brilliantly added a comforting diversion to the rather serious discussion, by quickly turning our attention to the need for some tea.

The interval of waiting for the return of the Indians went altogether too fast as we made full-day trips to places of local scenic and naturalistic interest, worked on various projects, gathered and cut wood, until the day came when the Indians returned with the message from the barrister regarding the meeting date and place. Leisurely we prepared for the trip to the railhead.

Our camps en route were fun, the weather mixed but mostly fair. I had some idea of what the subject meant when he said that his wife adjusted as readily to the wilderness as to metropolitan life. She was a skilled camp cook, capable on the portages and in canoe travel. We met a party of Indians on the way who spoke no English, and the subject's wife handled this with linguistic finesse. I learned that she had been employed as an interpreter in Montreal and as a translator of the written

syllabic Indian language developed by the missionary James
Evans in 1841.

The bonds of friendship build rapidly, especially when developed as mutual and significant ties. The hundred miles of
canoe travel to the railroad was far too fleeting. As my train
bore me back to my cabin on Lake Superior, I looked forward,
nevertheless, to the pleasure of more relaxed days. Fulfillment
of life posed many additional questions, but I was willing to
leave a number of them unanswered as insights yet to be gained
about wilderness living. The vicarious answers are scarcely ever
sufficient to the questions one poses about one's own life. They
must be lived for a solution.

8

Scrutinizing the Inscrutable Wilderness

ONLY INTIMATE and rather prolonged contact with the wilds seems to allow any significant revelation of its inner secrets. Perhaps it is that too many of us "have eyes but cannot see, have ears but cannot hear." We might also add that some have minds but do not allow full play of their faculties. Yet all of this, I am convinced, can, in most instances, be altered by assiduous practice.

In his capacity as wilderness guide, a friend of mine told me that one of his chief difficulties in pointing out wildlife to his patrons is that often they cannot see it even when its position is pointed out. Since the guide needs to be as quiet as possible to prevent wildlife hearing him, and as motionless as possible to avoid flushing wildlife into cover, designating the position of some creature from a canoe, or from shore, becomes continually difficult.

He has tried several methods of pointing out wildlife, none

of which have proven wholly satisfactory. Most wildlife is not too disturbed by seeing a canoe some distance away, so that one can get quite close to many creatures by employing the under-water paddle stroke, impelling the canoe without removing the paddle from the water. (See my book, *North American Canoe Country,* published by The Macmillan Company.)

One method used by the guide to signal the sight of a wild creature to his patrons was to wiggle his own stern slightly on the stern seat of the canoe, with the least apparent body movement. This vibrated the canoe enough to alert his patron in the bow seat to something he should see. Then, with an underwater stroke, the guide would slowly point the bow of the canoe dead on toward the wildlife. The slow turning movement of the canoe usually does not disturb—it is rapid movement that most disturbs wildlife.

A creature as big as a distant moose, the guide says, often cannot be seen by his patrons even when the bow is pointed dead ahead toward the moose. Wilderness shores have many large, black, upturned root systems that from a distance can be mistaken for a moose or a bear by the initiate. What also happens is that some creature seen by the guide has already stealthily slipped unobserved into the forest cover before it can be pointed out.

Frequently, one of the guide's patrons, not seeing the wild-life being pointed out to him, would excitedly say, "Where? Where? I don't see it," not realizing that in his eagerness he had made a number of disturbing body movements, usually the rapid swinging of his head, or the turning of his body from side to side. Any sound carries readily over quiet water.

Another method the guide used for designating wildlife was to think of the canoe's bow as twelve o'clock, no matter where it pointed, and then in a whisper, say to his patron: "Moose, two o'clock," or "Moose, eleven o'clock," or whatever the creature and its position on the imaginary clock dial were.

When moose feed on roots in rather deep water, it is possible, especially in the fly season, to paddle rapidly toward the animal while his head is under water, then have the canoeists freeze into immobility when the animal's head begins to come up. In this manner, one is able to approach close enough to get a full-negative image with a camera, using only a standard lens. The chances increase, of course, with the use of a telephoto lens, since the canoe can remain undisturbingly at a distance and still get the same full-negative image. It is not good pictorially to get *only* the animal contrasted against a patch of water. To associate the creature with his environment is greatly to improve the result, since the animal is then identified with his habitat, if only a segment of it. When taking a picture from a land position across water, one should, if possible, frame the creature through attractive vegetation. Or, use a picturesque backdrop of trees and the opposite shore, if available. The same is true when one is in a canoe, photographing an animal in the water, viewed toward the opposite shore. Long-focus telephoto lenses tend to pull distant vegetation up close to the animal. If the animal image through a telescope lens appears to be brought from 100 feet to 25 feet, the backdrop shore, say 800 feet away, will appear only 200 feet from the animal—a four-to-one factor of compression of subject that is worth remembering.

It is not unusual to find that a wild area of the continent has been traveled by canoe, snowmobile, with packhorse or dog team, or even on foot, for several weeks with no great amount of wildlife seen—sometimes none except perhaps a few birds or wild fowl in flight. This is particularly true with snowmobile travel and with the motor-equipped canoe. Once in the wilder-

"To associate the creature with his environment . . ."

ness, the snowmobile should be parked and travel done on snowshoes. And where the wilderness has been reached by canoe and motor, further movement should be with the paddle, the underwater stroke, of course, being used when nearing the vicinity where wildlife might most likely be seen.

Reasons for not seeing wildlife increase in number. If ever we have occasion to travel with a woods Indian, we will discover what these reasons are. In a canoe, for example, he will lose his respect for us if hour after hour we chatter like a magpie. Watch him. His ability to make no unnecessary movement or sound is astounding. He lets his eyes scan the shore without moving his head more than necessary. If he stops paddling, we can be sure some notable object has caught his attention. If we keep paddling or ask why he stopped, no answer may be forthcoming. He expects by his suspension of movement that an intelligent deduction will be made and that we will try to perceive what he sees or hears. Immobile, and with his eyes steadily focused on a particular place in the scene, he is likely to indicate without further designation an opportunity to see what he sees. When ready to paddle again, he will usually say briefly and in a subdued voice, *"muhekun"* (wolf), *"ochak"* (fisher), naming whatever creature he has seen, then silently continue on.

What generally amazes one when traveling with a wilderness-born, wilderness-reared, and wilderness-living Indian, is that he has the normal pattern of the wilds so established in his mind's eye that any slight deviation from the norm catches his attention. At one time while in camp with an Indian companion, I noticed well back in the branches of a tree what I concluded was a mass of dry black vegetation. To observe it more carefully, I went to a pack for my miniature field glasses.

In the meantime my Indian companion stood looking at it, a smile breaking out on his face.

"What is it?" I asked. "A squirrel's nest?"

"Wapistan" (marten), he said simply.

Not until I had accommodated the field glasses to my 20-20 vision did I recognize it. As we sat around the campfire that evening, I asked him how he had managed to identify the marten so readily.

Amusedly, he said, "Your squirrel nest moved."

This obviously was not all of it. Cars on the whole look alike to me, because I have no special interest in them. To a certain youngster in my village, all makes of cars are so different he can name the make a hundred yards away. To the trained eye of an Indian, martens are different in one way or another from a solid mass of twigs that might be as dark and shaped the same.

When Vilhjalmur Stefansson, the arctic explorer, lived off the arctic prairie in his early explorations, he used a pocket-size pair of binoculars to sweep the horizon for a possible sight of caribou. If he saw anything he could not readily identify with the small glasses, he used a high-powered pair to verify the individual objects. The optical practicability of this will be apparent; one goes from the *general* to the *particular,* and this is also the basis of seeing with the naked eye.

No doubt, one could provide material to fill several volumes on camouflage in nature, and its visual deception. The weasel's white winter coat with a tiny black tip on the end of his tail, for example, might seem to give him away to his enemies until we discover that it proves to be an attention diverting factor that hides the weasel. The black spot catches the eye, so that the white part of the weasel against the snow is not immediately apparent.

Scrutinizing the Inscrutable Wilderness

The wilderness traveler who sleeps through the first hour or two of morning daylight is not apt to see much wildlife. Also, if he gets into camp toward evening when wildlife might again be on the move as readily as it is in the early morning, the chances are that he will create enough disturbance in making camp to flush most wildlife out of the area.

Since there is a common, bad tendency to measure the success of a wilderness trip by the number of miles traveled, streaking through it, little wildlife is generally seen. To see wildlife, one should rise well before daylight and be in a blind, or sufficiently hidden in the various areas frequented by different creatures to simulate camouflage. A sandy beach where there is a grassy meadow, lily pads in fairly shallow water, and a tiny stream running into a lake will usually have moose feeding there at daylight. The place should be explored for fairly fresh tracks beforehand to learn if it is being frequented by wildlife. A mid-afternoon camp would also allow one to reach such a beach area in a blind toward dusk—a time when moose are seen just as frequently in these places as they are early in the morning. Such places are generally found deep in some bay and are most often missed because they are off the direct canoe routes.

The shortest distance between two points, we are told, is a straight line. It is not the most direct route to seeing wildlife. Skirting a shore in a canoe ten to fifty feet from the water's edge can bring a far greater return in interest than the common method of cutting across the middle of a lake and scanning the distant shores. However, if a good vantage point is had over much water, a ten-minute search of the shores with binoculars can bring into view wildlife that subsequently can be approached from cover.

On various canoe trips, I have pitched a camp on a fairly large lake, broken camp the next morning and traveled all day on the same lake, skirting the shore, purposely arriving at the same camp spot at day's end, to use the same tent stakes. Some of the lakes, of course, because of their size, required several days to weeks in skirting the shores, when intervening camps had to be made. If this suggests a sameness to some in scenic travel and wildlife interest, then try it and enjoy the surprise. Because it changes direction each time a point or two has been rounded, the route along the shore has the effect of one going on and on into new country. The return route seems no less strange by virtue of the altered angle of view.

Much of what happens in the wilderness, we need to realize, is beyond ordinary scrutiny. *Obscurity* from average travel is the phrase that describes it. An opportunity to see a bear swimming and to observe the strange fact that he swims with his forelegs stroking the water to propel himself while his hind legs stream out horizontally behind him, is not a common observation, as we might presume. Much of the wilds is thus obscured.

If one baits a bear on a small island with highly odoriferous substances, such as decayed fish entrails or burned sugar, one might have an opportunity of seeing him take off in the water for the mainland.

The streaking wilderness trip mentioned does not, as a rule, provide time for these deliberate experiments. Watching otter on a slide, or seeing them play with one another as they swim down a lake, is not going to be a common sight if otter tracks or other evidence are not first discovered. There may also be a need for baiting in the region they frequent.

These few examples might point up the need to approach the wilds in a manner different from the casual one. A mile of wilderness examined with predetermined knowledge of animal habits will reveal a hundred times more signs of wildlife than innumerable miles traveled by canoe, packhorse, or on foot, if those miles are only roughly and remotely scanned. The need is for a *questing eye*. It can be said that a tremendous amount of wildlife sees the average wilderness traveler.

It is generally assumed that seeing wildlife in the wilderness is a mere blundering onto creatures caught unaware. Sometimes it does happen. Breaking camp so early in the morning that breakfast is eaten by the light of a campfire offers a far better chance for seeing wildlife than doing so after dawn. Silently paddling around an island and coming slowly into view of a grassy bay is best done as the first rays of daylight begin to light the water. The curtain then is usually lifted on whatever creatures are in the area. One can, however, spoil it all by a single spoken word or the bumping of a paddle against the canoe.

If the canoe route reaches the more northerly forest areas of the Canadian provinces or into the territories and Alaska, the chances are very good that woodland or barren ground caribou might be seen. The day you come upon them by canoe, if your journey has been long enough to transcend some high latitude, will be especially exciting, because caribou are so often the indicators that transition from the wildlife seen farther south to that which tends more to be on the watershed of the Arctic has begun. Earlier in the century when caribou herds were large, and long travel by canoe or dogsled brought the first sight of the vast herds during migration, the effect upon the traveler could only be described as colossally exciting.

Sight of the first caribou, moose, bear, fox, wolverine, lynx, marten, fisher, mink, weasel, or other wild creature obviously has an intensifying effect upon the success of a canoe journey, or other wilderness travel.

The Wilderness Life

Toward fall the great waterfowl migratory flight begins. The stages of the movement allow feeding periods over the long flight south. It is possible, therefore, to come by canoe upon a wild rice bed in the overflow of a meandering stream where the ducks are so numerous as to give a moment of fright by the booming sound of their rise as you flush them.

The field glass and the camera, as suggested, obviously will be indispensable on any wilderness journey, be it canoe travel, winter sled travel, with packhorse, or on foot. But the real complement to this equipment will be the advance information acquired of the region to be traveled. A small manual on each division of subject can make the difference between the casual approach and that which gives a wilderness journey lifetime significance.

That the natural forces and their cryptic elements will always remain just a step beyond man's full knowledge goes without saying. The mysteries and complexities of nature's various functions and just the plain *why* of all natural phenomena stump scientist and layman at some point of limiting comprehension. Imponderable as the multiplicity and complexity of the natural subjects are, we are left with the choice of either devoting a lifetime to the scientific study of a particular phase, or simply browsing for knowledge here and there in the wilderness for pleasure and amazement. Such browsing can be less haphazard with the aid of pocket manuals.

Most of us devoted to the wilderness are, I presume, in the casual observer category. And yet, there are times when the special interest becomes a spell so alluring, some of us in varying degree tend, for the time being, to be captive, amateur scientists.

On the other hand, there are those who travel through a wilderness region and intentionally choose not to become

Ducks feed in great numbers in the wild rice beds.

familiar with the most conspicuous of natural phenomena. The proverbial hunter who shot a settler's black mule, believing it to be a moose, and drove a thousand miles showing it off draped across his car hood, testifies to learning inadequacy. As the absurd story goes, it was a natural mistake in identity, except that the spectators viewing the "moose" wondered about the animal having been shod. On the same score, evergreens are simply "pines" to many people. Misidentification of a species does not, of course, alter its growth, or even perhaps greatly destroy its pleasurable effect upon the observer. But to make an acquaintance who might become a friend and not even know the acquaintance's name, be the subject a human being, an animal, or a plant, seems a bit unsociable, or at least alien to life's special advantages. To know more about anyone or anything would seem to add luster, intimacy, and pleasure.

General information about wilderness rather than scientific knowledge is, no doubt, enough for pleasure and utility, but to gather even this with a time limitation is no small task. A mere blushing acquaintance with some of the first impressions experienced on a wilderness journey can open up for the acquisitive mind a Pandora's box of interest. Successively developing phases of interest are certain to accrue from trip to trip.

One advantage in observing the nature of vegetation is that, unlike wild creatures, it will not on inspection run from sight.

I am not suggesting that the average wilderness traveler should undertake an elaborate program of botanizing; but simply to see, touch, and know the name and uses of a few dozen trees, shrubs, and plants can give one a familiar feeling toward the area.

On the initial wilderness trip, say in northern Ontario, the flora will probably look something like this: a dense forest basically of black and white spruce, balsam, and jackpine, with

Scrutinizing the Inscrutable Wilderness

a few cedar at the water's edge. Moose maple, mountain ash, and a vast number of low shrubs, such as Labrador tea, will be a part of the deciduous growth. While there will be a white pine and red or Norway pine here and there, sometimes even a stand of them, be prepared to find that the mental picture you might have entertained of regally walking through aisles of pines will be realized. The forest will seem jungle-like in the density of its growth. If you are on a canoe journey, the chances are that you might on some shores have the chore of clearing brush from an area to gain even enough room to pitch your tent and to move about freely.

Bough beds are traditional, but in this day most of us will be sleeping on air matresses. To hark back to that era when the balsam bough bed was the traditional means of softening the ground, I hope that you now will cut only a few boughs and thus help to save the forest. Tuck in a sprig or two of balsam where its fragrance will become symbolic of your nights in camp.

Identification of the balsam will be the easiest of botanical lessons. The fragrance of a few needles crushed in the hand may prompt you to wonder why anyone would bother with Chanel No. 5, when Balsam No. 1 would most delectably arouse one's olfactory sense. Its short needles grow alternately on the twig like a double-row of teeth on a comb. Also, for ready identification, balsam bark along the whole trunk will have numerous resin-filled blisters, which, if pricked and pressed, will squirt out a stream of fragrant, syrupy resin.

Intermixed with the balsam, even perhaps predominating, will likely be the black and the white spruce. Unlike the double needle row of the balsam, spruce needles emanate all around the stem; they have a fragrance, though not the olfactory delight of the balsam. The quality of wood in both spruces is better than the balsam, for example, if you have to make a spare paddle.

However, the selection for the paddle should be white spruce, since it is superior to the woods of both black spruce and balsam.

While the white and Norway pines will be seen scattered here and there, the predominant pine in the areas of the spruce and the balsam will likely be the Banksian pine, better known as jackpine. The chances are that if you are looking for choice campfire wood, which is also fragrant when burnt, your eye will catch the standing dead jackpine nearest to your camp area. When that long siege of rain comes, and nothing in the forest appears to be dry enough to burn, you will find that a quarter inch below the surface and the dead jackpines on the uplands, the dead cedars which project out over the water, and the dead tamarack in some swamps, the wood will be as dry as the desert to kindle your fire.

Because of something different in the soil, the climate—who can say just what—conifers and other growth having their own characteristics will be indigenous and dominate other particular areas on the continent. Some woods, such as the pitch or candlewood pine in the eastern United States, are so loaded with resin that a section will burn like a candle, or a torch. To me the most fragrant of all pines when its wood is burnt is the piñon pine of the Southwest.

Wherever we chance to roam, an investment of an hour with a manual for identification beforehand can provide the protocol needed to move among these stalwart tree figures of the forest. Such a manual can be so pleasing in the first endeavor that others on shrubs, flowers and lesser plants or lichens, on mammals, on wild fowl and song birds, on fishes, on reptiles—even on insects—will be sought. The knowledge gained from such texts, when related to subjects in the field, could identify one as having viewed the inner sanctum of nature's house.

9

Wilderness Art, Campcraft, and Science

IT SEEMS THAT by virtue of circumstance, the individual who undergoes a transition in his way of life and residence from an urban center to a natural environment usually finds himself acquiring an interest in some phase of the arts or crafts. The reason may be obvious. As to the crafts, he is by necessity, in most instances of wilderness environment, required to be a maintenance jack-of-all-trades. Once an individual becomes involved with tools and their use in the wilds, the manual pursuit can reach a point where the lay person on occasion achieves the skill of a craftsman.

Individuals who previously lived sedentary lives often discover that they possess a potential dexterity not before considered possible. The advantages go beyond the mere physical reflex use of the hands. There is also an effect upon the central nervous system, a habituation toward shaping things, which in time becomes so pleasant in the manual process that restlessness is felt unless something in the field of crafts is taking shape. This, in a broader sense, can have more import than we realize. Unless one continually combines some kind of manual effort with intellectual effort, the reflexes of either mind or body seem to lose something. The "use it or lose it" concept has been quite well determined. Even the therapeutic value of following a craft has been fairly well established clinically.

Those who through retirement take up a more naturalistic and leisurely life find that a need for diversion from their former life faces them. An interest in a craft has a way of supplying part of this. Not only is this true in the actual creating of various items, but the making of them tends to invoke other interests. For example, the individual who ties flies as fishing lures generally not only becomes interested in fishing skills, but discovers the feeding habits of various fish species, a step that could well lead to a study of ichtheology, a fascinating natural science. A woodworking craft usually encourages an interest in the properties of various woods. This can inspire the gaining of knowledge about how the woods grow, an interest that in turn could lead first to dendrology, then on to the subject of dendrochronology, the science dealing with the study of the annual growth rings of trees in determining the dates and chronological order of past events. We see in this ascending order of knowledge that the craftsman becomes brother to the scientist.

Tradesmen who accomplish their work skillfully and fast have achieved facility through long, thoughtful practice—the emphasis here being on *thoughtful*. The amateur craftsman is often capable of doing the same excellent work but doing it more slowly, sometimes the only difference between the lay individual and the tradesman.

There is no doubt that a certain manual dexterity needs to be developed to bridge the gap more effectively from urban to outer-suburban or wilderness living. The individual who has been pursuing a craft as a hobby will likely come closer to making the transition than the individual with a fat pocketbook who has had all home maintenance done at a price. But this is not always so. We have to consider the potentiality of each individual. In short, out of a number of manually inexperienced people, some will do better than others on the very first effort, and a rare few will actually show prodigious accomplishment. Those using tools for the first time who seem inadvertently to risk committing mayhem upon themselves can scarcely be expected to bridge the gap from a sedentary life to one requiring manual skills, without some readily available manual help. This help can sometimes be found, but it would seem that here a minimal effort should be made for such help, if only to bridge the physical handicap.

If stressing manual effort seems to be a required theme in bridging the gap from city to country, it is because the very essence of a successful wilderness life rests on our ability not only to do things with our hands, but to *derive pleasure* from doing them.

Natives of long residence on the perimeter of the wilderness base their first appraisal of a newcomer in their midst primarily on his ability to carry on a manually capable existence, and secondly on the qualties of his personality. The reason for this is that the small wilderness settlement becomes somewhat communal because of utilitarian necessity. A time will likely come when one will need cooperative manual help, and the time will also come when one may be required to give it. Should one happen to show some special manual skill, the chances are good that one's standing in the community will rise significantly.

In much earlier days, I looked with particular respect toward a certain man who could swing an ax with equal dexterity right-handed or left-handed. While undercutting a tree for directional felling, he was able to stand in one advantageous position to undercut the tree and merely reverse his handhold on the ax without changing his stance to cut through the tree on the other side for felling. When on a canoe trip at a later time with this axman, I asked him on which side of the canoe he most preferred to paddle, he facetiously said, "Mostly on both sides." Such accomplishments make better canoe men as well as better axmen.

Adroitness goes far beyond maintenance alone in the wilderness. A sustaining interest over the years is scarcely ever acquired without some manual program. People who make things with their hands—items for which counterparts can be bought—sometimes suffer confrontation with that element of the populace who appraise everything on the basis of whether it is commercially worthwhile to make. When we think in terms of price only, value is lost.

I believe it was Maxfield Parrish, the artist, who found diversion and a kind of inspiration by leaving an unfinished painting on his desert studio easel and going to work in his private workshop nearby, where he derived as much pleasure from making the picture frame as he did from painting the canvas which was to go into it.

It is doubtful, however, that bridging the gap from city to wilderness can best be achieved by pursuing a specialized manual interest alone. Obsessively pursuing a hobby could finally result in that satiety which takes the joyful edge off the craft. Yet, I am inclined to believe, after much observation of this subject, that manual pursuits can maintain interest as consistently as intellectual pursuits.

Perhaps the most successful pursuit is a hobby that has been, or tends to be, implemented with a broad, diversified background of interest. The artist paints a subject, only the subject, and nothing but the subject; yet the influence of long-garnered knowledge and broad vision in other fields somehow inadvertently get into and improve his graphic expression. Hobby, manual craft, graphic art—whatever the focus of interest—ought thus to be complemented with a great deal of accessory living, if it is to provide the main arch in a successful bridging process.

THE SCIENTIST

There is another approach to the arts and crafts in wilderness which concerns some individuals in part and others at considerable length. It is that of an individual's scientific interests. I refer chiefly to the various scientific instruments that can be applied to wilderness phenomena—those concerned with meteorology or weather forecasting, celestial navigation, advanced photography, and others. One can be well informed on weather by listening to a radio, and to this I have been readily able to defer. I have not, in dispensing with gadgetry, been able to bypass some of the technical instruments by any such singular process. When it comes to traveling by various means in wilderness areas, for example, I have a weakness for wanting to determine at all times by scientific means where I am, where trails have led, and where they lead back to point of beginning.

I must therefore confess to having derived a tremendous amount of pleasure from applying high-precision equipment to natural phenomena. When I can measure the altitude of the sun or other celestial body with a sextant and find my exact position where there are no other guideposts, when I can use the sextant to find the time of day and day of the year and measure the height of a waterfall as well, I have not wandered away from nature in favor of gadgets or mechanization per se, but feel that I have joined the wilderness in its most elemental sense. (See my book, *The Wilderness Route Finder,* published by The Macmillan Company.) When photography, for example, permits one to manipulate the chemical and physical properties of light with color filters, polarization filters, electronic flash synchronization in complement with daylight, etc., bending these factors to nature, I am unable to disassociate them with wilderness.

Perhaps even the full-fledged scientist will move his laboratory to the wilds. We can hope that when he then undertakes to solve some of life's intricate problems as a result, he won't forget that he is already environmentally in a great natural laboratory to which he can join his efforts.

THE ARTIST

If the aspiring artist is properly advised to go to the garret economically for his success, then I would try to intercept him on the first few steps of the narrow attic stairway, and suggest that he go to the wilderness perimeter instead. For there he has infinite subject matter, and can also devise props, as well as having the best solution to his economic problems. A simple one-room cabin set on the wilderness perimeter could give him the potential advantages enjoyed by the established master, if we also presume that he has an insatiable lust for artistic expression. Without a strong urge for expression, he would, of course, fail, whether working in a garret, a wilderness cabin, or an urban studio. The aspiring artist is not one who says that some day he is going to paint pictures. He cannot keep from painting. If he were thrown into jail without the materials of his medium, he would spend his time scratching images on the wall with his fingernails.

THE PHOTOGRAPHER

There was a time when the camera was regarded only as an accessory item on a camping trip, used casually for the perfunctory record. What has happened to photography in recent years makes it such an institution of artistic expression that one no longer simply buys a camera but a whole *system,* usually at least two camera bodies, several lenses and filters, an electronic flash, and other pertinent accessories.

Whether interested in photography as a hobby, as an art, or as a means of earning a livelihood, the wilderness dweller has in this medium perhaps one of his greatest aids to the enrichment of living. The natural environment as subject matter for photography holds out an invitation for self-expression as great as any other medium or pursuit. It can also be a means of livelihood which could permit the individual to subsist wherever he chose. A suitable contact with an advertising agent can provide the link needed for the commercial disposition of both black-and-white and color prints of wilderness subjects, defraying living expenses, where otherwise this might incur a hard-to-solve economic problem near the wilds. What is perhaps most significant at this time is that a vast amount of illustrating material is bought by advertising agents from amateur photographers.

This does not mean, of course, that the amateur photographer with just a camera and the casual approach to obtaining pictures can sustain his economic position in the wilds. He needs a fundamental knowledge of photography and a substantial amount of equipment, which is expensive. He can, however, begin modestly and expand according to his means.

Photographing wildlife is probably the most intriguing challenge to the wilderness photographer. Patience will likely be his greatest asset. Stalking or baiting animals, discovering their habitats, shooting pictures from blinds and by remote control will be the daily test. The 35-millimeter, power-driven camera, remotely controlled by a radio-trip device functional at about 200 feet, will bring the most certain success. An almost extravagant use of film will likely be another great asset. Power-driven cameras taking a number of exposures to get the single impressive pose will allow the critical selection of exposures. Picking the best negative from a number is a matter of having a good wastebasket in one's head, or simply a process of separating gold from dross. Film for wildlife photography should be bought in bulk and loaded into cartridges by the photographer himself. This greatly reduces the cost and allows a freer use of film.

Both flora and fauna pictorially adapted, in either color or black-and-white, present no lack of subject matter in the wilds and have high appeal to advertising agents. A flower, a Rembrandt lighting of a sunlit, mossy area in the deep forest—most any subject caught in effective lighting can produce an eye-catching picture of commercial value. Large color prints of natural subjects for framing also have high appeal to the general public.

THE WRITER

An editor once told me at a luncheon discussion that "We need more writers on wilderness." I was anxious to press the point as to why there were not highly competitive numbers of them. "It apparently isn't the easiest subject experience-wise to come by," he replied, "since most outdoor interest lacks scope beyond hunting and fishing."

The writer on wilderness, it seems, has the least need to go to the garret. A simple cabin in the wilderness or on its perimeter, a grubstake, a ream of paper, and a fistful of pencils, or preferably a typewriter, should leave only one remaining element necessary—an avid desire to observe and write. Impulsively, we might presume that experience has to come before the aspiring writer will have anything to say. He can, I think, take exception to this on less than empiric grounds. One of the most fascinating accounts of wilderness I have read was by a writer who left the buzz of New York City, drove to northern Ontario for his health, purchased a run-down cabin on a lakeshore site, and described the vicissitudes of "getting away from it all," without previous wilderness experience.

Here, we no doubt have the greatest chance for the uninitiated reader bent on a like enterprise to identify with the writer. Rare is the individual, regardless of aspiration, who has not thought of a cabin habitat off in the silent places of a wilderness and speculated about how he might fare without an experienced grasp on the environment. To live from day to day in the pages of a book with someone who, by trial and error, is doing it, or has done it, fighting adversity, reaping pleasures, sensing the myriad aspects of wilderness, is almost akin to being there, for it is the reader doing these things in a sense, not so much vicariously as potentially in the projected future of his own personal plans.

If "your style of writing is you," the same premise can likely be applied to the content of your writing. Although I do not write fiction, I owe a debt of gratitude to the early writers who wrote that fiction not based on feasibility. The wilderness was depicted as a fantastic nether world, a region of great mystery, of ghostlike creatures. The adventurer fought the grotesque beasts of the forest hand to claw and fang. Timber wolves rimmed the night campfire, where survival of the campers was possible only by hurling firebrands at the encroaching animals. Great wolf packs were fought off while shooting from the barricade of a tipped-over dogsled on the lake ice. Moose, having driven a victim up a tree, kept him there for days during rutting season. Bears raided camps in the presence of campers and by a fortunate diverting appetite ran off with large hams and slabs of bacon in lieu of devouring campers. Wilderness travelers soaked by days of rain had fingers too numb from cold to build a fire for warmth. Weasels leaped from tree ambushes to the throats of humans to suck their blood. The *Windigo* (Spirit) stole canoes at night, leaving trappers to wander aimlessly through the forest over the long traverse to the outside, with odds against survival ten to one, and so on ad infinitum.

Surely, if these things happened, adventure subject matter would have no end for writer and publisher.

But, ah me, they are not so! They belong to that breed of spooky horror stories which have their origin in abandoned old homesteads. One reads them with great credulity, profound pleasure and trembling, when young. Oh, to be young enough again still to believe them! Romance! Adventure! I rue the day that they would be denied publication.

Some magazines still presume to continue this fiction. If you write it, you won't need wilderness experience, vicarious or real. Simply let your conjecturing mind wander into the realm of deception and absurdity. At the same time, prepare for censure by the wilderness veteran and certain oblivion for what you write. "We need more writers on wilderness," true; but even the callowest youth of today, seeking wilderness adventure, does not believe these old wives' tales, and little of the newer vintage in fiction, if he has learned anything at all about the wilds.

This may seem like disillusionment to some, yet it is not. Coping with wilderness is adventure. To repeat Stefansson's phrase, "adventure is the result of incompetence," and incompetence is the result of false premises and little experience in the wilderness. Wilderness is challenge and realism, a test of the intrepid, kind and benevolent to the competent, cruel and impersonal to the disregardful, romantic to the imaginative, fulfilling to the thoughtful and considerate, inscrutable yet sufficiently revealing to the searching mind. It calls for prose to depict it realistically and profoundly, and poetry for beauty and feeling where prose is inadequate.

Perhaps the greatest demand upon the wilderness writer in the future will be accounts of natural phenomena critically observed, free from established doctrines or the fantastic preconceptions of the earlier fiction writers. We live in a questioning age when the depiction of phenomena has to be rational and artful, superseding fiction no matter how infallibly we have heretofore regarded it as fact. The observations of early writers are on trial for credibility, as are those of today, and as those of tomorrow will be. It is a process of knowledge and wisdom moving along on its evolutionary course.

It prompts every writer to so observe his subject that he will live less by conjecture, fictional fraud, or superstition, and more by what seems from his best effort and viewpoint to be fact, feeling, romance, and beauty. What we consider currently to be well-known fact becomes more and more moot with added knowledge, we realize. But there is an empirical and sane premise on which we have to rest for the moment, and by which we have to live.

Perhaps there is no department of human endeavor that has more conjecture, more fictional fancy, more deception and illusion than the writing on wilderness subjects. The purpose has been, of course, to augment the artificial and pervert the natural for sensational appeal, where perversion, the writer hoped, would not be detected.

Fortunately, we are entering into a revelatory age of writing and publishing. Editors and people of learning today would not accept without question, for example, the long-held false notion that man has a sense of direction. We know from exhaustive experiment that he walks in circles unless he has some directional clue to orient him. (See *The Wilderness Route Finder.*) If the archives are packed with writing on the wilds that has been conjectural and erroneous in context, perhaps the chief responsibility of today's writers is to edit by rewriting the fantasy that was once purported to be fact.

Also, when we write of wilderness today, we no longer consider it a thicket in a ravine, but as part of the whole, vast, cosmic scheme that is an evolving force. Ecology as a significant part of living was not understood through most of the past. Now it has come everywhere into its own, more formidably perhaps from having lain fallow for writers all these years when it was, nevertheless, growing critical. It is a term that the writer on wilderness will find looming before him as an inextinguishable warning light.

But the writer who is only concerned with despair over wilderness ravage misses the boat where reader interest is concerned. I repeat: there is still a great wilderness remaining. Growth and the amending forces of nature are inexorably persistent. Ravage will in time be corrected by those forces to make the world bloom wholesomely again and again, following periods of desecration. Future generations and their writers may well look upon the interval of ravage we are now experiencing as just another period in history between the time when rivers once ran crystal clear and a new age when they will again run clear. The process where man's role is concerned may be contingent upon the influence of the scribe—whether conservationist, scientist, poet, artist, or romanticist—who has discovered the grand magnitude of wilderness.

10

The Seasonal Wilderness

SPRING

IN HIS CLASSIC VOLUME, *The Private Papers of Henry Ryecroft,* George Gissing exclaimed, "Oh, for one more spring!" Perhaps this was the same sort of lament as George Bernard Shaw's "Oh, to be eighty again!" Most of us look with great anticipation toward spring, and think of it as imparting the tenderness of new bloom, of youth, of new hope and beginning. One individual theorized that he should go to that latitude which had the earliest spring, and then follow the sun's declination in order that spring might be prolonged. But he found more variables in the seasonal change than were determined by the sun's altitude above the horizon. Spring rainfall came irregularly, giving vernal splendor in some northern regions, while others farther south, though warm, still lay dormant in winter's drab garb because of delayed rains.

Nevertheless, latitude and the sun's declination do, to a great extent, become governing factors. Spring arriving in a warm latitude might tend to deceive the wilderness traveler as he plans to go farther north. One degree of latitude is roughly sixty-seven statute miles. It is not unusual, for example, to plan a Canadian wilderness trip when spring is in full promise, say at North Latitude 45° or farther south, and on arriving at about North Latitude 50°, discover lakes still frozen and a snowstorm sweeping across the landscape.

As one goes from the desert into the mountains, altitude can also be a governing factor. It has been estimated that every thousand feet of change in elevation may be comparable to a difference of three hundred miles of latitude, both in temperature and indigenous growth. Also, of course, there is the influence of coastal waters.

Winter is long in the northern latitudes, which makes the coming of spring there more welcome perhaps than in the lower latitudes. As temperatures begin to rise, the white, snowy stretches of northern lake ice start turning grey, then grey-black, until one wonders if some dark pigment was loosed in the water at freeze-up time. It is, of course, not a pigmentation but a crystallization or candling of the ice, which creates by light refraction this illusion of grey-black; every crystal when lifted and examined is transparently clear, and when melted produces clear water.

The Canadian jay is the first to recognize the short northern warm weather season. Before the dark ice has gone, the young jays have already been hatched. And it is not unusual to see the parent birds foraging for their young in a snowstorm. While the Canada jay and the chickadee find a seed supply in coniferous forests, it is well to keep feeder boxes stocked to brighten the early spring season around a cabin.

There is something almost spectacular in the spring breakup of the ice, not particularly in the ice movement itself, but in

"While the Canada jay and the chickadee . . . brighten the early spring . . ."

the fact that one often goes to bed with a bleak view of grey-black ice lighted by the moon, to awaken in the morning and see the sun flashing upon whitecapped waves of open water. The sudden disappearance of the billions of compacted ice crystals is nothing short of astounding.

Even then as the waves wash the shore, one does not over-extend confidence, for the lake, if becalmed, can again freeze over, and subsequently be covered with twenty inches of snow in a single storm. One knows, however, that winter has pretty much lost the contest with the sun's imposing northern trend, and that the unseasonal affront, if it appears, will go away about as quickly as it arrived. Enormous, spawning northern pike now lie along the shore in shallow water. As the break comes in earnest, great V-shaped flocks of geese begin winging over. They might land on the immediate open water to await the breakup in the lakes farther north, or in great numbers head for the salt marshes of James Bay.

It is time for the canoe to come down off the rack where, inverted, it has rested all winter. The chances are that the first canoe trip will be to the nearest settlement to put in a fresh supply of provisions, something that was not possible in the transition period between candling ice and first open water.

Bear, scrawny-looking from their hiberation, now ravenously hungry, are easily baited in for photography. You might see them catching fish in the shallow overflows or digging for roots. Starved as they now are, they cannot indulge in caprices of appetite. They need food, whatever is edible, and they need it soon.

Moose will be dropping their calves before long, and the ruffed grouse will be heard drumming in the forest. Mink will fish the first open trout streams.

Once the snow has gone from the open areas, that stimulating

"Bear, scrawny-looking from their hibernation . . ."

"Mink will fish the first open trout streams."

fragrance of the vibrant earth is strongly in evidence. Chipmunks that fed from one's hand the previous fall are now aroused from their long hibernation under the snow and reappear seemingly unaware of the time that has elapsed.

Deep in the forest where the snow hangs on, prolonged refrigeration can be had far into warm spring days. This is especially true in the perpetual shade on the north side of an overhanging rock rim.

Spring in the wilds calls for early rising in order not to miss its incredibly rapid unfolding. The dormant blanks created by winter are filling in everywhere with both wildlife and plant growth. It is a gold rush of opportunity for various creatures reoccupying territories which most of them abandoned through the winter.

Woody growth shows the first signs of budding, and you are now discovering that members of the deer family no longer yard in the over-browsed, dense forests and marshes. Tender buds are supplying their urgent need for fodder. The deer begin to flesh out, and by the time the wearying fly season arrives, the animals will have built up sufficient resistance to withstand the onslaught of summer insects, which will for a time make them lean again.

SUMMER

From the middle of June through July and about half of August can be considered the extent of summer in the northern wilds, with a great deal of variation on both ends of this spectrum of time and weather, which is also, of course, as mentioned, affected by latitude, altitude, and somewhat by coastal influences. The sun has now climbed high enough in the North to crowd almost two days of daylight into one. In the higher latitudes daylight is almost perpetual. Vegetation is on a growing spree, appearing to take full advantage of the short warm season. Members of the deer family can be seen on the waterfronts; moose, escaping as best they can the swarms of insects, have little more than their heads out of the water as they feed on roots of water lilies. Caribou have been moving north out of the scrub forest to their summer feeding grounds on the arctic prairie.

The northern summer has its profits and losses, depending on how you view it. The warming temperature brings flies, which can become so intolerable as to drive you indoors. If, say, wilderness travel is contemplated early to avoid the insects, then there can be an overlap of seasons when winter may reach beyond its average limit. If the margin of safety is passed on this winter weather hazard, then you are generally precipitated pell-mell from cold into the hot fly season by the sudden change.

Perhaps the fly season of June and July can best be termed the cabin period. It is not necessarily the retreat of the timorous. Life in a wilderness cabin simply has the advantage of allowing the more urgent regulation of daily life. You can, for example, be out on the water during those hours of sunlight and wind when insects are kept at a disadvantage; and you can be back in the cabin when there is no breeze and be screened from the onslaught of mosquitoes that move in at eventide like a plague. The tent, properly protected with mosquito netting, does offer partial escape, but some in-camp duties have to be performed with a handicap. Repellents, head nets, and gloves have their drawbacks.

Those of us who spend long periods in the wilderness usually take a certain pride in coping with seasonal adversities, no matter what they are, treating them as problems to resolve by whatever available methods. But sometimes the coping reaches such extended proportions that the advantages gained by being in a certain environment do not seem to be worth the investment of corrective effort.

The resolution involves a kind of migration.

Early in my wilderness life, I discovered, while carrying a pack through the North, that within fifty to one hundred feet from shore of very cold bodies of water, such as Lake Superior and Great Bear Lake, insects fought a losing battle with the temperature close to shore—summer's heat being held back by the temperature-chilling influence of the water. During the summer heat, camps have thus been made tenable for years on such cold water shores, either on mainland or on island, which allowed closing the seasonal gap caused by flies and heat, permitting year-round wilderness travel and living.

AUTUMN

Mixed feelings plague many people when the fall of the year rolls around. In those areas where winter is long, there is deep regret that summer is waning. With most of us who are close to the wilderness in all seasons, autumn is the preferred time of year. The fly season has tapered off. If an early frost should come some night in the North, as it frequently does, it can spell doom for most insect pests until another year. Autumn temperatures moderate to that coolness which induces a lust for physical activity. Autumn on occasion can be in the air even before the vegetation loses its green and begins its spectacular coloration. It is the time of year for that long-anticipated canoe trip, for a packhorse or backpacking trip. The heat of summer might unseasonably invade early autumn, but not very often.

If one could follow the sun's declination to prolong autumn, as mentioned for spring, this might be the seasonal zone over which to move latitudinally to reap a continued harvest of autumnal beauty and pleasant activity.

For wildlife, autumn seems to be the greatest season for food and comfortable living. The deer family no longer suffers the agonies of swarming insects. The abundant, natural food crop leaves little to be desired for wildlife. Waterfowl are in the wild rice beds. Bear are fattening on berries, fish, and rodents, although at times the meagerness of the berry crop, caused by late spring frosts killing the blossoms, forces bear to scrounge heavily to gain enough body fat to carry them through the coming hibernation period.

Wilderness trips in the North, kept within a zone from North Latitudes 45° to 55°, should begin in August and end when there is the least risk of being frozen in for the winter. The time span between start and finish of a trip in this zone averages about seven weeks—seven weeks of the most pleasurable recreation in the year. One cooks outdoors with an appetite for food, over an open fire that lends both cheer and a comforting warmth. One enjoys the feel of clothes. The cooling of temperatures during this period is so gradual that when the colder late autumn days and nights come, one's physical adjustment to the temperature has been so well made that an amazingly limited amount of clothing is required. Summer lethargy has gone. No canoe water route seems too great, no portage trail too strenuous. On the packhorse trail the animals seem to move with greater animation, and there is no end to fodder for them at most travel altitudes. The backpacker lives with a lust for the trail. His every step is mercurial, each encampment a memorable event.

WINTER

When the autumn weeks have passed and a wintery chill is in the air, lucky is he who has made the autumn-to-winter temperature transition in the wilds, for winter will not then seem to him a weather hurdle. In late autumn, as in spring, there is a period when travel is suspended—the ice too thin on the lakes; the open, unfrozen moving waters too frequently interrupted with forming ice barriers. The canoe goes up on the rack, and from out of the cache cabin comes the toboggan, the dogsled or the snowmobile, to be serviced as needed to make it ready. There have been days of wood gathering just before the freeze-up. Now in the interim between seasons, when travel is curtailed, the wood will be sawed and split for the kitchen range, and into longer segments for the fireplace and heater, then stowed under cover from the soon-to-arrive snows. The fragrance of resinous wood hangs over the cabin camp, as stimulating as the fragrance of desert bloom following a period of rain.

The interval without travel offers, as well, a time for leisure and rest. Perhaps one has not been aware of it but the intense autumn activity, while greatly conditioning muscles, has also taken its energy toll. One needs, as it were, to lie fallow for a while, even like the bear to put on a little winter fat.

Soon the ice will have thickened enough for travel, but not yet. The few earlier freezes are insufficient to hold the subsurface waters in check. Areas yet unfrozen consequently are caught by the wind and break open the frozen areas, sending plate-glass sheets of ice slithering up on shore. Whitecaps on the reopened lake seem exultant, as though on a last spree before being imprisoned under the ice. Some morning after a still, cold night, you will awake to a dawn so hushed, the whole world will seem to have gone into suspended animation. Though day, it is like the night couched in sleep. Winter's stillness has come in earnest.

Now you want the sky to remain clear, for then the night will very likely be cold enough to freeze the ice to a safe thickness for travel. It is hoped that no early snow will fall to cover the thin ice and insulate it from the cold air. The weight of a heavy snowfall on thin ice causes the underwater to be forced up and to seep under the snow layer, where it does not freeze and creates slush that delays travel. The slush freezes on to your footgear, so that you walk with cold and leaden feet; or you are encumbered with sled runners that do not slide, and snowmobiles that become immobile from slush frozen in the treads.

These are not critical problems but simply periods of delay. Come what may, the wind finally packs the snow. But the snow will afford little insulation when the sub-zero temperatures do come, for they penetrate this crusty snow to make the ice progressively thicker—three to four feet on the lakes of southern Canada and the northern United States, seven feet in the upper Arctic. The season now settles down to its usual conformity. Peace and quiet reign over the northland. On occasion nature will run rampant even in the grip of winter, when the blizzard breaks the quiet and roars with defiance—but on the whole, quiet is the normal state. When the blizzard subsides, the silence by contrast is so deep, the sound of an ax splitting wood seems to rend the air like the crack of thunder. Now and then, a tree trunk affected by the extreme cold gives a report like a rifle shot. A red squirrel will chatter deep in the forest, or a chickadee utter a friendly note. Indoors there is only the cheerful sound of burning wood, and perhaps the whisper of a steaming teakettle.

Some night as this peace reigns and the meaning of the phrase "the silent places" is deeply impressed upon one, there will come from the distant hills the howl of a timber wolf, first with loud crescendo as if near, then trailing off as if in despair, lost in the infinity of space.

11

The Wilderness Indian

AFTER MORE THAN half a century of travel and living deep in the wilderness, I have failed to understand fully the variousness of man's indigenous habitats and habits—what prompted his choice of environment, why certain groups are on the whole happy with the wilderness environment while others dislike it or fail to cope with it. We too often come up with the absurdity that an aversion to it involves a civilizing process, presuming, more willfully than knowledgeably, that a long cultural evolution has developed one major ethnic group "out of the primitive."

The American Indian and Eskimo living in the wilderness do as well, on the average, with the outboard motor and snowmobile as the whites. We can thus rule out the belief that certain groups live a wilderness life because they are not the evolutionary product of a long cultural and industrial civilization. What still remains in the broad appraisal of the nature of

The Wilderness Indian

Indians and Eskimos living happily and very capably in the wild areas where they are indigenous is that after a full taste of the urban environment, they often return to the wilderness life, a move invidiously regarded by too many people as a return to the blanket. I know of no genealogy among my forebears where there is a trace of American Indian, although I would hope there could be; yet after a few weeks or months of urban indulgence, I too have a strong urge to wend my way back to the natural environment.

Does our own long association with the natural environment tell us how the Indian feels?

When there has been opportunity to discuss their preferences of habitat and life-style with Indians, their decorum often prevents them from speaking out freely. The age-old awkwardness of confrontation between Indian and white still hangs like a pall over the complete freedom of interacting expression. But I have found that where the lure of the wild is strongly demonstrated among whites, where whites have come sincerely to respect Indian culture and wilderness values after considerable wilderness association and competence, the Indian will accept the white and regard him as his brother. This is not a matter of feeling or displaying the common, casual, affected empathy toward another race, but a case of having enough knowledge of Indian culture to qualify the relationship. Disingenuousness can build the highest and most forbidding ethnic wall.

Where for ten years as a wilderness director of two youth camps I had carried on a program of enlisting Indians to teach their culture, a time once came when a party of some twenty Indians, none of whom I knew, traveled a hundred miles from a reservation to perform a ceremony making me a "blood brother." Sincerity plays the biggest role in the American Indian's attitude toward individual whites. The Indians apparently considered that I could truly identify with them because I had genuinely embraced their culture for the edification of the young.

Sitting intimately in groups around a campfire in the wilds, around their fireplaces in urban centers and reservations, they will reveal that the boomerang life of the Indian from reservation to city and back to reservation is essentially a matter of appraising life's values as Indians find them to be. The materialism that has fascinated so many of us, regardless of race, fails to offer most Indians the peace, calm, and profound satisfaction needed for their life-style. The designation coined early in history by the Indian, "crazy white man," was derived from the white man's obsession with industry. The employment price industry demands for its material standards, the Indian asserts, is too high to pay. This is why so many of them will agree to work only a day or two each week for their current needs. The anomaly here is that they actually are a vigorous, not a lazy, people.

What has long been regarded as stoicism in the American Indian behavior pattern is simply an absence of petulance, as we may observe by an experience I had back near the early part of the century in Canada's Ontario wilderness. At a waterfall portage an Indian family came upon me preparing my evening meal. The late afternoon sky being clear, the cool autumn air delightful, I had delayed pitching a tent but planned to do so somewhere in the immediate area for the night. I was frying walleyed pike fillets, the fish having just been taken from below the falls in the swirling riffles. Also, I had a large pan of cornbread baking in a reflector oven nearby, before a flash-flame type of fire. Some hot coals from the reflector oven fire had been raked aside for frying the fish.

A reluctance to intrude on my privacy seemed to be written

"... an Indian family came upon me preparing my evening meal."

on the faces of the adult members of the family, although they had no choice but to land where I was, in order to ascend the steep portage trail nearby around the falls. Two youngsters of about three to five years hung back in cringing embarrassment, cuddling some tiny husky puppies.

The family, I learned, had intended netting a few fish in the eddies below the falls for their evening meal and camping somewhere in the general area for the night. A wide chasm existed in oral communication between us, bridged only by their few words of English and my own fewer words of Cree. I believe that they, in respect to my having preceded them to the site, would have bypassed me and gone on over the portage had not the good fortune of the now baked cornbread circumstantially intervened. I cut two generous pieces and spread slathers of peanut butter and strawberry jam on them for the youngsters, which proved enough to break down their timidity. This also helped to drop whatever barrier might have existed between the parents and me. For the parents I poured tea and set out the cornbread and fried fish, refilling the frying pan with fillets.

Without a word, I was gracefully elbowed away from the fire by the mother, who made it apparent that I should eat while she continued the preparation of the meal. In the meantime, the father and I reset the gill net and soon pulled it for the additional fish needed. A dozen or more in the net were turned back into the water, since we had too many for our supper. In those days using the gill net was legal, but it was later outlawed to prevent its abuse.

A friend of mine, widely traveled in foreign countries, said that he avoided the tourist bureaus' group travel package, so that he could spend his money living close to families in various countries and cultures. This method of gaining an insight into

"A large flock of snow geese rose from the water . . ."

the complexities of people interacting with people in a different culture from one's own took on special meaning as I now was taken into the confidence of this Indian family.

Evening moved in gently, although the roar of the falls was a bit disconcerting, as it usually becomes when one remains too long in the presence of roaring whitewater. Autumn's coolness being upon us and the insect season no longer a concern, we decided to move out of the wind to the far end of the portage trail to camp on a level area of a lakefront, enjoying increasing relief from the roar of the falls with each muffling bend in the trail. A large flock of snow geese rose from the water as we came to the lake.

To avoid flaunting my rather pretentious equipment, I sought a spot well away from their camp to pitch my tent. It was an unusually fine tent, made by David T. Abercrombie of New York,* now no longer in business. I unrolled and inflated an air mattress, on which I spread a down sleeping robe made in Scotland from Sea Island cotton and eiderdown from Iceland. And so it went on through my whole equipment bought only at great financial sacrifice on my part, at a time when affluence was a river that did not flow past my door.

How much actually was gained with my sophisticated outfit compared with that of the Indians? They set up a coarse canvas wall tent, laid down a mattress of balsam boughs, and rolled out rabbit-skin robes. After all, whose sleep was the most sound, the most peaceful?

As we sat around the evening fire, I found that I could not long assume the ground-sitting posture of the Indians without a cramping discomfort. I shifted about while the Indians sat relaxed, contemplating the magnificent surrounding forest.

* Not associated with a present-day firm of somewhat similar name.

The Wilderness Indian

These Indians were not living in the tempo of sportsmen or tourists bustling with activity on a vacation, but people long habituated to the environment.

Other than the canvas tent, guns, knives, two cooking kettles, an ax, a fishnet, and a few sundry items, their equipment and most of their clothes were derived from the wilderness.

In a conventional, vocational world, one must admire a skillful use of tools. What becomes apparent in watching wilderness Indians is not only their skill but their prodigious extension of the use of a very few tools. Their incredibly versatile skill with the crooked knife is an example. This item was traditionally sold through the centuries by the Hudson's Bay Company (see *The New Way of the Wilderness,* Macmillan Publishing Co.). Most often it was made by the Indians themselves from worn-out files, forged in the heat of open, outdoor, charcoal fires. Birchbark canoes and snowshoes had long been made with little more than the crooked knife. For the Indian it was a great stride forward from what he made do with as tools earlier. At a sponsored Indian exhibition at Mille Lacs Lake, Minnesota, before a crowd of spectators, I watched the making of a birchbark canoe and a pair of snowshoes with only flint tools. The stones of flint had been gathered from the immediate environment as a part of the exhibition, and were fletched on the scene to produce the required cutting edges. It was, of course, a planned demonstration, the Indians there normally using the steel tools they had made or bought—especially the crooked knife.

The transition among Indian natives from a primordial culture to one affected by modern industry, from flint knives to those of steel, from the birchbark or skin *mekewap* to the fabric tent, seems natural enough. But when one sees deep in the wilds the cast-off suit coats of the white man replacing the buckskin shirt, the transition disturbs one's sense of romantic, if not ethnic, cultural values. And yet, one can say, "What is wrong with the warming comfort of a cast-off wool suit coat?" Incongruity, I suppose. Feeling the lapel of a suit coat worn by an Indian friend, I asked facetiously, "Smoke-tanned buckskin?" "No," he said, "Harris tweed."

I was awakened in my camp near the Indians early in the morning by a distantly muffled gunshot. Shortly, the father returned alone in the birchbark canoe holding a snow goose. I thought the flock we had flushed out of the bay the night before had flown to far distant waters. The goose had been shot to be cooked for breakfast, the Indian man and woman considering that it was their turn to supply the provender. I wanted to spend more time with this delightful family and managed to get the goose meal put off until evening somewhere farther along the water route; so with the assistance of the mother, we panned out a breakfast of oatmeal, bacon, and stewed dried fruit from my own pack of provisions.

Gesture, pantomime, the helping hand—you do not know just what builds it—but the bond of growing friendship can become ever apparent when oral communication is a handicap. I played with the yougsters, getting down on all fours and growling to imitate creatures they had visually known well even at their early age. I stood at the water's edge and made a loon call by the trick of cupping one's hands and blowing through moistened thumbs. As loons answered, the youngsters laughed with great amusement, and the parents smiled approvingly.

After we had broken camp and continued on our journey farther up the lake, the father gestured that we pull into shore. He took his gun and stalked inland along the lake. Soon I heard another shot, and presently we retrieved a second snow goose from the water. It seemed, as the father indicated, that one small goose was not enough for five hungry people. A straight meat diet is not at all like the meals one conventionally eats, in which several complementary food items comprise a meal. We consumed a large portion of both geese, although I must admit we were all a bit too well fed.

Roast goose? Not in the expedient fashion of the Indian's cooking on the wilderness trail. A large kettle was hung over the fire with salted water. When a tumbling boil began, pieces of goose were placed in the boiling water, only one piece at a time, so that boiling did not stop. The mother tested the meat for tenderness from time to time and finally lifted the kettle to a place where we were to have our meal. I had baked two bannocks to complement the meal, but we did not eat them, saving them for a later time. With small pointed sticks, we served ourselves pieces of goose, and as a beverage, drank the broth from the boiled goose meat. Outside of metal cups and the large kettle, there were no dishes to wash.

There was an appropriate wilderness simplicity in eating this way. Once the kettle was empty, the mother set a pail of water on the fire to heat, into which she added wood ashes. (Lye from wood ashes and fat made the soap in Colonial days.) Our cups went into this lye solution, which saponified the residual goose fat and made the cups easy to rinse clean with lake water. As I went to the lake for a pail of water to rinse our cups, I kept turning over in my mind the notions of convenience, expediency, and economy of time, and the cumbersomeness of too many utensils that normally in white man's way have to be washed. What would the daily, totaled dishwashing time add up to with the multiplicity of dishes in the average conventional family's lifetime? I shudder at the thought.

My speculation on Indian wilderness expediency was not to

end with this mealtime episode. Within a few days I departed from the enriching association with the Indian family to go on my own separate wilderness route, to follow my own procedure, although now to be influenced by the expedience and leisure of Indian methods of living.

The bond of friendship between us had already tightened. When one of the youngsters learned that his family and I were parting, he ran and hid behind a tree to prevent my seeing him cry. This hiding of emotion is built into the Indian character early. To vent such feelings in the open was thought by the youngster to be shameful. When I sought to console him, he angrily beat me off with his fists. But as the family moved down the lake in one direction, I in another, both youngsters waved ceaselessly until they were out of sight. I was a bit sad for a day or two.

12

Wilderness Guile

How many of us, through inadvertent choice of occupational or social position and circumstances, live lives of silent desperation, we shall never know. The dreams of today are too often shattered in the unrealized adventures of tomorrow. Some do scale the walls of the fortress of economic or social obligation and risk adventure in the open. One can even laud the Walter Mittys, whose vicarious experiences outdo the most inconceivable actual adventures.

What is to be said, on the other hand, about the fortitude, or to use a term restricted to male campers, the "virility" of those who profess a great interest in the wilds and adventure, yet claim that they do not undertake such activity because they want a good bed, and don't want to eat off the ground or carry heavy packs over portage and mountain trails?

On this premise I can understand the success of saunas and other businesses that provide "passive gymnastics." For a fee one can attend these health spas or exercise salons and, while lying prostrate, have someone else or something else (many "gyms" boast elaborate exercise machinery) actuate one's joints, rather than having to flex one's own. Would these same people not say that the cold morning shower or the walk on a cold winter day would have refreshing merit if only it were not cold?

In rationalizing what may seem to be an apparent envy on the part of the phlegmatic, we make a mistake if we presume that the individual who declares he must have the comforts of home in the wilderness and objects to strenuous physical effort really wants to experience the wilderness. May I insist that his premise not be taken too literally. An example of this might be contained in the conversation I overheard between a woodsman in the process of building a log cabin and a spectator.

"That looks like a tough job," the spectator observed.

"It's tough, but I enjoy it," replied the builder.

"Seems to me that kind of work would make a person coarse."

"I suppose it does make a person a bit rough."

"Then why do you work at it?"

"To get the cabin built and keep from going flabby."

The episode might have ended right there in offending the spectator, except that the builder apparently was a man of empirical wisdom, or perhaps even a psychologist of sorts. Before he had scarcely taken another breath, he called down to the spectator, "Say, would you mind handing me that gouge and hammer down there in the corner?" (Lincoln, you recall, made a friend out of an enemy by asking a favor of him.) The spectator had to climb a half dozen rungs of a ladder to hand up the requested tools to the builder. As he was about to descend, the builder asked, "Would you also help me roll this log over with that canthook so that I can notch it for the corner?"

"What's a canthook?"

"It's that gadget hanging on the wall to the right of you."

I was observing profound skill in handling human nature, the amelioration of antagonism, and the dispelling of illusion. I had brought the builder's mail by canoe and was soon to depart on my own chores down the lake, but I lingered long enough to hear a few more remarks exchanged between the builder and the spectator.

"The way you straddle that log wall, you would be a natural as a log cabin builder. Are you in a hurry, or could you give me a little more help?"

Three days later, passing by in my canoe with another mail packet for the builder, I saw the spectator poised high on the ridge pole, holding the top end of a rafter in place, while the builder was notching and spiking it into place on the wall. The spectator waved to me from what could be a precarious position, imparting a confident smile.

Many people live their lives needlessly alienated from desirable activities. To take a line out of context from Alfred Noyes, they ". . . stand by the wall, watching the fun of the victory ball." They will not discover their capabilities until presented with the proper challenge, or compelled by some unforeseen circumstance to participate in the unexpected activity.

The initial effort to make a wilderness trip can end in discouragement due to bad weather, going during the peak insect season, or some other indisposition. The reaction can even build up to distaste for the wilderness on the part of novices, and on occasion create resentment toward the initiator of the trip.

One cannot, of course, criticize anyone for wanting to have a good bed. Spartanism is not the greatest virtue. There are extremely lightweight, three-quarter-length air mattresses that most of us find ample when they are properly adapted. There are full-length, deep air mattresses that can compete in comfort with water beds or beds that the finest hotels have to offer. An eiderdown sleeping unit spread over such an air mattress would certainly offer better cover than the best blankets, the use of which has always seemed to me comparable to wearing a hair shirt. The preparation of food in a camp need not be makeshift or catch-as-catch-can. Fine meals can be had outdoors with a moderate amount of skill. Wilderness travelers, of course, do not have to pamper their appetites. In over a half century of wilderness travel, I have not eaten a meal off the ground, although, to risk a pun, I see no earthly objection to it. Picnickers have done so traditionally.

An almost physical invalidism, wherein one does not wish to carry a pack, portage a canoe, hike over a trail, pedal a bicycle, or otherwise flex one's muscles, is obviously a problem of having neglected physical development over a considerable length of time, generally that period following active youth. Lack of exercise has the well-known serious potential, as we know, of ensuing illness. To begin exercising vigorously following such long physical lethargy could involve coronary disaster. The building-up process needs to be gradual. In time, as muscle-flexing increases in amount, the desire to exercise increases, until a day comes when physical activity becomes so essential to comfort that life does not seem wholly complete and comfortable without it. When one reaches a point when there is actually a craving for exercise, the benefits become extraordinary. To be continually lethargic is never to know the exhilaration of optimum health—a logic to be comprehended only after physical conditioning.

Camping incompetence derives most often from the psychology behind the adage that a little experience is a dangerous thing. It is strange that an intelligent man is willing to admit his inexperience in nearly all things except the very few which concern virility. It is therefore rare on this basis that any man admits a lack of campcraft knowledge and skill. The male camper who takes a short vacation once each year frequently finds it incredible that he should be asked what his competence in camping is. The female camper, to whom virility is not a problem, is far more likely to seek advice. Long exposure to all weather and every camping condition, preferably with a competent teacher, should be the only criterion on which one should judge for oneself whether the short vacation camping period had given him significant procedural merit. Campcraft suffers because it is believed to be so elementary that it requires no substantial study or highly developed skill. One may hope that for his safety or camping perseverance, the vacation camper is never tested for survival skill under stress or left to his own resources beyond the sunny-day, short-duration lark.

Wilderness orientation is not only a matter of acquiring a knowledge of campcraft, but also one of knowing how to cope with the wide range of elements as well.

Annual trips into the wilderness by canoe, packhorse, or on foot have averaged for me about seven weeks, usually from the last of the fly season until the first ice would begin to form near shore. Winter trips were organized to start well into freeze-up and end when midwinter snows became too deep for expedient travel. The extended periods have provided some high points of adjustment. One develops an increasing competence and naturalness in the daily routine as the weeks pass and as the weather varies or becomes suddenly adverse. Also, trips of such duration involve more than the easy courses, where government wilderness services have not smoothed the way.

Those of us who for various reasons have the good fortune of being able to spend long periods in untracked wilderness usually find as much delight in traveling with a novice as companion as with someone of experience and competence. This is especially true if the initiate, while deriving enjoyment, also shows potential and willingness to learn. On the other hand, an initiate who, by guile, leads his experienced wilderness companion to believe that he is competent when he is not, will offer a double challenge.

The first step in resolving this duality of guile and pretext is to allow the novice enough latitude in his own presumptuous efforts to learn the hazard and futility of doing things impulsively and without competence. Yet you must be able to snatch him back from the brink of disaster, or from the lesser consequence of common blunder. If his impulsiveness is simply a strong desire to do his part it becomes commendable, if at the same time you can prevent possible harm. If he holds up his end satisfactorily, and even from day to day manifests improvement, it is fairly certain that before the trip is well along, you will have a companion of rare, developing ability.

How much potential, unexpressed knowledge exists in the world, we shall never know. It must be vast. In the novice one now and then finds suppressed prodigious capability.

Sometimes emulation is carried by a companion into rivalry for achievement. When that rivalry carries with it a growing competence, the chances are at times that the master even learns from the student. When rivalry becomes a manifestation of the upstart's overweening confidence you may be compelled to use stringent methods of initiation.

One of my companions labored under the illusion that he had a sense of direction. When I periodically checked our course with a compass as we were heading back to camp through a forest region after exploring a height of land, he said with a wry smile, "Why don't you put that damned thing in your pocket." He did not disregard instrumentation over long travel on the canoe route, however; it was just that he would not forgo entirely his presumption that he could walk four to five miles on a straight course through a dense forest area instinctively without a compass, where directional clues were zero. Visibility in the forest where we were hiking at the time was very limited. The sky was heavily overcast, and with no apparent prevailing wind to orient us, there was need for a periodic check of compass bearing.

"Okay," I said, "why don't I put it in my pocket and see how we come out." I nodded that he go ahead.

I followed, now and then checking his direction with the compass, taking care not to let him see me do it.

He held a rather commendable course for a short distance, then began to veer slightly to the left, but not enough to give notice that he was straying. It was enough of an error, nevertheless, that in another mile it brought us to a tamarack swamp which we had not encountered when outbound on a compass course. This swamp he decided to skirt to the left, which was the first really notable error. Had he skirted it toward the right, he might inadvertently have corrected some of his directional error. When he was satisfied that he had reached a take-off point from the swamp on the opposite side, his orientation became quite bad. He was now heading almost ninety degrees off course. In about twenty minutes more of travel, he was again veering to the left and in his travel had described about two-thirds of a circle.

Whether he was becoming a bit apprehensive then about his directional ability, I was not certain, although he said, "It seems a hell of a lot farther back than it was coming."

"Maybe we are just a little tired," I commented deceptively.

About three-quarters of an hour later we came out to the waterfront, upon which he exclaimed, "Finally!" and gazed apprehensively up and down the lakeshore, trying to determine which direction to take toward our camp. Nothing looked familiar.

Had he taken either direction along the shore to our camp, we would have spent the night without supper, with a need to build some kind of bivouac in the rain, because the overcast held off no longer, and as we later learned, became a three-day rain. One direction would eventually have led to our camp, but the shore had a many-fingered irregularity that would have required several additional hours to skirt, taking us well into the night before finally, having survived the hazards of stumbling through black night's invisibility, we could have reached camp.

Every time there had been a radical change in direction, I had made rough calculations in a diary notebook, using watch and compass. My companion did not see these jottings, being ahead of me and rather excitedly bent on proving his sense of direction.

At the shore he looked at me, somewhat chagrined, and said, "I must admit I don't know in what direction along this shore our camp is located."

It was raining lightly, but I said, "Let's sit down over here on this rock formation—I want to show you something." A drizzle fell on the pages of my notebook, where a scrawl showed lines in various directions designated by rough estimates of the time elapsed.

"I feel kind of foolish," he said, after examining the sheet. "Judging from where your line stopped, we must be here," he pointed. "And if that's the case, we have to cut through the woods again to travel the shortest way to our camp. Right?"

I agreed, and said, "Here. You take the compass and lead us back to some chow."

He was off with the compass and the eagerness of a hound dog headed for home.

"One more thing," I called out. He stopped, so obligingly solicitous I was almost embarrassed.

"What's that?" he wanted to know.

"Until we get something to eat, don't put that 'damn thing in your pocket,'" I joshingly said.

In less than an hour he reached the waterfront within about two hundred feet of our camp, which I thought was a compliment to him, to the discoverer of the compass, and to my time-directional scrawl.

13

Rescue

CANADA HAS SET some restrictions on allowing the inexperienced to make wilderness trips of certain latitudes, or into very remote areas, in order to prevent such persons from getting lost. Nevertheless, in recent years fortunes have been expended by the government on plane flights searching for the missing, where the situations were such that they could still be alive. On occasion I have been intercepted at points of embarkation on canoe, backpack, packhorse, and dogsled trips, by the Royal Canadian Mounted Police, requiring my qualification proving that I was competent to travel in the outlying wilderness.

As in every other department of life where there is some physical risk, the wilderness does take its toll. That the wilderness is benevolent toward its own is as true as that the wilderness can be impersonal in the disposition of those who fail to survive its rigors. The fact that those who succumb in the wild areas of the world, whether there for recreation, adventure, exploration, or war, are seldom found and are not likely to be, is for many people difficult to understand.

We who spend long periods in remote wilderness areas which have large wildlife populations can testify advisedly that seldom do we come upon the remains of wild creatures—so rapid is their assimilation by nature's various processes. Even creatures that drown in rivers and lakes soon surface, drift ashore, and undergo the same rapid mutation, basic in the natural cycle of degeneration and regeneration occurring on land.

Early in the century those of us lingering momentarily on the wilderness fringe were now and then recruited to fight forest fires; also, if competent to travel in the interior, we were asked on occasion to search for lost persons. Fighting fires was a chore one did not relish too much, although duty here was, of course, ever apparent. Besides, there was no alternative— enlistment was compulsory then as it is today. On the other hand, to be asked to find persons lost in a vast wilderness had the alluring elements of compassion, romance, and adventure about it.

In those days on the Canadian National Railway there were a great many wilderness siding signal stops, most having tiny trading posts. Some of these sidings today have developed into substantial settlements because of outlying rich mineral deposits, pulpwood cutting, and recreational advantages. Earlier the region was an uncharted wilderness, the posts patronized largely by Indian trappers. It was in that period that Joe, an Ontario Indian friend of mine, and I selected such a railroad siding stop as the jumping-off place for our canoe voyage to the North.

When we arrived and were about to pick up a few extra food items at the railroad siding trading post, we became aware of two fashionably dressed, middle-aged couples engaged in serious conversation with the local trading post owner and, as near as I can recall, either a provincial policeman or a Mounty. They were discussing a lost canoe party of two young men in their late teens. From the conversation we overheard, we presumed that the policeman planned to organize a search party of some Indians from the upper lake region. Each couple, it turned out, had a son on the canoe trip from which they were long overdue.

For a moment, the parents, in their grave concern, turned to us. On telling them that we were headed out on a similar canoe trip, we became two more young adventurers who would be risking life in what they saw as the untracked, hazardous wilds of the North. When the trading post owner explained that my Indian friend and I had previously been through that same north country on a winter's dogsled trip of three hundred miles or more, their concern for us was quickly dispelled.

"Joe," I said, "the good lady here is afraid you are going to get lost."

"Last year I get lost," Joe said.

"Where?" I asked.

With a grin, he replied, "Winnipeg."

Ordinarily, this might have been amusing, but not here to four anxious parents. Joe, uncomfortable with the King's English, remained aloof from the conversation, choosing to wander casually around the store. At this juncture, the boys' parents asked me if we would undertake a search for their lost sons, employing whatever Indians we needed to assist us in the upper country. I called to Joe for approval. He and I would surely have found it a moral obligation to search for the pair to the limit of our own not too plentiful means; but out of the clear, to my utter dismay, Joe asked the parents, "How much you pay?"

"Joe," I said, "you're mercenary." One might be aghast at Joe's seeming indecorum, until one understands more intimately the early woods Indian's point of view, which was simply that he did not regard being delayed indefinitely in the wilderness as cause for alarm. Capable of sustaining himself by living off the land, where he was at home, he expected the same competence in others. It amounts to the old joke, "Indian not lost. Trail lost. Indian here."

Congenial and adventurous, Joe usually went along with whatever plans I might have projected. Staggered by the pay we were to receive per diem during the search, plus a substantial reward if we found the canoe trippers, Joe and I immediately became amenable to whatever the search might entail.

The policeman, after questioning us at some length, seemed to think that we were capable of making the initial search; but he added that if we did not get results within a reasonable length of time, a rather vague projection, we were to report out, so that the search might continue.

The parents in the meantime were to head for Winnipeg on the first way-freight train affording passenger service in the caboose, then to remain at a hotel through the search to await further word from us. Their manner, dress, and extraordinarily liberal offers of cash led us to believe that they were among the more affluent and were not making sacrifices beyond their means in trying to find their sons. As Joe later in an off moment put it, "Jesus, they rich, eh?" We might have deferred accepting the generous advance cash payment bestowed on us until we had proved our worth; but Joe came up with the speedy alternative that—translated from the Cree and paraphrased—suggested: "A bill in the hand will be no handicap in the bush." Also, we had to resolve the possibility of paying Indians whom we might need to hire, if available, to augment the search, and to reprovision ourselves at an outpost, although with firearms and fishing tackle, we planned in that early time to live largely off the country. The parents had told us, "Whatever you do, spare no expense or effort."

Our packs loaded into the canoe, Joe and I were soon headed north, bucking a more than thirty-mile stretch of whitecapped water. Almost two days of hard paddling, terminating in heavy rain squalls the second day, brought us to the upper end of the lake, where we found a good camp spot—one showing much use by Indians. We also found some signs that indicated it had apparently been the camping place of the missing canoeists. It was a natural stop for anyone after the long stretch of paddle-wielding.

What bore this out as also having been the canoeists' campsite was the fact that earlier at the post, in collecting pictures and identifying data, I had roughly sketched in a notebook the kind of footgear the canoeists had worn, and, among other things, had noted the color of their canoe. Along the sand beach and in the soft ground back from the shore, we identified footprints, almost obliterated by rain, as impressions of the sole and heel patterns of the footgear that had been described to us. Joe called my attention to a small piece of flat rock partially buried in the wet shore sand that had paint scrapes on it of the same color as that of the canoeists' craft. At this early stage of the search, these bits of identification were of value, of course, only for possible comparison later with other of their used campsites we might find. In my notebook data I had also written down a detailed list given me by the trading post owner of some special food items the lads had purchased from him. For once, I hoped that they had been careless enough campers to have strewn identifying wrappings or empty, labeled cans around their campsites. Indians in those days scarcely ever purchased canned or processed foods.

One additional valuable item of information had been acquired. The canoeists brought with their equipment only a small hatchet, which the trading post owner told them was scarcely adequate. He said that what they needed was a two and one-half pound cruiser or pole ax, which he could furnish them—advice for some reason they saw fit to disregard. According to the parents, their sons had little or no experience in axmanship. This shortcoming we felt might give us a clue to distinguishing the shallow cuts of a hatchet from the deeper cuts of the pole ax used by Indians and other competent woodsmen. In fact, at the very next camp spot, we found evidence of this hacking with a hatchet. Also, there were tent stakes cut much too short for good mooring, along with various minor manifestations of limited knowledge of campcraft.

We now believed that we would be able to follow the canoeists' general route quite well—a more or less directionally natural water course of connecting lakes and rivers to the North. As we continued on, our searching around for their subsequent campsites in the immediate river segment became simpler, although this advantage was soon to end. What made tracking the canoeists easier for us along the river was the slowing of travel due to portages around rapids and falls that required more frequent camps. As for coming upon signs of their route in the narrowing river waters, Joe said their camps now were so plain that finding them was as easy as stumbling over a lazy dog. I tried to be the wilderness sleuth through our whole search, but I had to admit that Joe, Indian-trained and wise in Indian lore, was to the end always an observant step ahead of me. At McCrea and Pushkokogan lakes we had difficulty finding any of the canoeists' camps—both lakes being intricately broken up with numerous deep, dead-end bays and prominent points, as well as islands, and the lakes themselves spreading out raggedly in all directions over an area of several hundred square miles.

At the upper end of Pushkokogan, we ran onto some Indians headed, as I recall, for Fort Hope Post on Eabamet Lake, a widening of the Albany River, at about North Latitude 51° 30′, West Longitude 88°. Six Indians, constituting two families, were in the party. Questioning them in their native tongue, Joe learned that they had not seen the canoe trippers. But if we would arrange a rendezvous, they would, on their return from Fort Hope, let us know if anyone in that region had seen the canoeists. I promised payment as inducement for their efforts.

In the meantime Joe and I struck out on several likely canoe routes which might have lured the missing canoeists into false escape routes. We proposed to keep the total distance of these routes limited to the canoeists' approximate travel time schedule. Whenever the waters became rather complex, we stopped at high noon so that I could make a sighting on the sun with a sextant, and thus at least have a latitude line of position to use as a coordinate with whatever shoreline we were on, to help us keep the search systematically oriented for later reference.

The Indians, on their return from Fort Hope, reported at our rendezvous that the canoeists had not been seen at the Fort, nor were there signs of the canoeists having been at any of the used camps en route. To expand the search area, we now sought to hire both Indian parties traveling in two canoes; however, only the members of one canoe were able to accept. We assigned them to search again, but in more detail, the vast region of Pushkokogan and McCrea lakes, a big task in itself, and arranged for a second rendezvous. If the Indians were unsuccessful, we planned to have them search still other possible routes west of those Joe and I would cover, providing they would agree to do so.

The conclusion of their long search, as well as ours, which continued in the meantime, revealed nothing. With Joe's linguistic help we discussed every conceivable possibility. At this point nothing seemed to make sense. If the missing canoeists had upset in their canoe and drowned, we or the Indians certainly should have seen the floating craft. (Swamped cedar or canvas canoes float bottom up. Aluminum canoes of today, nonbuoyant except for their flotation chambers, float right side up when swamped.)

The search thus continually included the possibility of seeing a swamped canoe, or one beached. Also, there might be a chance, of course, of seeing a pitched tent. Before leaving the immediate area, a more diligent search was made for previously used camps, keeping in mind the identifying material we had. A task such as this might seem to be a fruitless one, and sometimes is, with endless shorelines; but due to the ruggedness of this Precambrian shield country, readily accessible campsites are relatively scarce.

It became evident at this time that the search would have to be expanded beyond what we had at first considered as within the lost canoeists' most likely travel area and time schedule. Again setting a rendezvous date, we had the Indian party search the waterway farther to the west, wherever they would find a plausible route over which the canoeists might have strayed. At the same time, Joe and I searched Greenbush Lake to the east, and then proceeded northeastward at about North Latitude $50°$ $55'$, to probe further, reaching likely routes. And on one of these routes we came upon the first significant signs of the lost canoeists.

The routes led through two small connecting lakes. Near an

outlet at the second lake, we came across a little-used campsite that showed distinct evidence of the lost canoeists' camp methods, readily distinguished from long-used Indian encampments.

Encouraged by this discovery, Joe and I were now undecided whether, in order to expedite the search, we should try for an earlier rendezvous with the Indian party searching to the west, or continue our search east and northeast into the lake and river country which drains into the Albany River. We decided to go it on our own to save time, considering that if we found the canoeists in poor condition, the sooner help came, the better chance they had of survival. Some of the routes we probed were through connecting creeks and obscure trails. These we soon abandoned when no camps were found.

We now had fairly good proof from this previously used camp that the canoeists were wandering aimlessly and would likely be found somewhere northeast of this region. In this instance, however, we hoped that they had not in some roundabout way blundered into the Albany River itself—a major route of river and expanding lakes continuing for about six hundred miles to James Bay.

I might mention here in passing that it is not entirely to the discredit of the canoeists that they became lost in these complex water systems. Choosing them for their canoe trip from the railroad northward, apparently by some recommendation, was not surprising, since here we have widespread, indescribably grand and infinitely varied canoe waters, mostly with rockbound shores forested with spruce, balsam, jackpine, and lesser deciduous growth. Off to the west is the Berens River, picking up its source in a multitude of streams, finally to merge in a splendid, rapids-punctuated river that empties into Lake Winnipeg some two hundred or more miles west. To the east is that strange chain of substantially large lakes and rivers that form the Ogoki drainage, working its way for several hundred miles of multiscenic grandeur toward the northeast to join its waters with the Albany. Farther off to the north are the Severn and Winisk Rivers, picking up countless tributaries in one of the strangest of all waterways; while to the northeast, similar in its drainage but with larger and fewer tributaries, is the Attawapiskat, as well as a number of other rivers, all eventually spilling into Hudson and James Bay.

The brief period allotted to the lost canoeists would have allowed them to see but a small part of this vast canoe country. Joe and I had planned on about seven weeks for our canoe voyage in this region, which to us also seemed extremely limited.

One morning just before noon, when Joe and I were keeping an eye open for a good lunch stop, we came to a series of rapids, and finding no immediate area suitable for a stop, due to the rough terrain, we made the several short portages around the cascades. At the foot of the last portage and cascade, we saw, drawn up rather precariously on a large, smooth Precambrian bedrock shore area, a damaged canoe, but with no immediate sign of a camp or campers. Looking around, we discovered a roughly pitched, badly sagging tent back in the woods on a higher elevation. The roar of the whitewater had drowned the sound of our approach. As we neared the campsite and shouted, a haggard, tearful, emotionally wrought-up young man, whom we recognized from a picture and description as one of the lost canoeists, hurriedly came stumbling out of the tent toward us. We were soon able to calm him, and briefly got his story. His immediate concern was for his companion, who, he said, had badly injured his leg and could not walk. Inside the tent, I found the injured lad suffering both physically and mentally. The canoeists had no idea where they were. They had been living on fish alone for some time, they said, but after losing their tackle in one of the rapids had not eaten anything for days and were undergoing the additional pangs of hunger. We learned that they had somehow drifted into one of the rapids, had upset in their canoe, and were able to recover only that equipment which floated.

If I had been concerned how Joe would meet the emotionally overwrought canoeist when he first came toward us from the tent, Joe's behavior soon allayed any qualms I might have had. What impressed me was that Joe—no doubt capable of extraordinary survival ability under the same circumstances—did not look askance at the canoeist, but took him by the arm and laid a comforting hand on his shoulder. The commonly presumed ethnic difference between the Indian and the white man was absent in the test of compassion. Rather, a mutual youthful empathy existed that was heart-warming to observe.

Joe quickly got a fire going, cooked some gruel, and fed the starved canoeists a very small amount at a time, to prevent them from suffering the severe cramps that occur when food in substantial quantities is taken on long-empty stomachs.

We pitched our own tent and got both of the lads bedded down in our sleeping robes. Night temperatures were now becoming quite cold. Since their bedding was still damp from the upset in the rapids and the ensuing weather had been too wet to dry it fully, Joe built a big fire well out on the bare rock shore to speed up the drying, and then re-pitched their tent. Meanwhile I examined the injured leg. It was not only black and blue but also swollen from the contusion, and obviously had a fracture of the tibia about six inches below the knee. Fortunately, the break was not a compound fracture. I chopped out a billet of wood from a dry cedar and split it into a variety of thin and thick splints, and with strips of cloth cut with a knife from an extra garment, along with caribou moss, managed to get fairly good support for the factured bone.

The lads were in too weak and overwrought a condition from their ordeal for us to attempt the return journey immediately—even though we knew it meant that their parents would be putting in extra time of anxious waiting.

One of the ironies was that while I made some casts with a rod and reel for fish in the riffles below one of the cascades, I hooked onto the fishing tackle the canoeists had lost. Somehow, their rod and reel had been driven down by the fast water to the lower end of the cascade, while the straggling fishline drifted loosely into the riffles to get caught on my spoonhook. It is fortunate that the canoeists had been in possession of their fishing tackle up to the time of the upset almost a week earlier; otherwise, considering the plight we found them in, they might have perished.

We now had four mouths to feed and a considerably reduced supply of store-bought provisions on hand. Joe set out in a canoe with a 30–30 carbine and a small-gauge shotgun to replenish our supply, returning with some ducks. The next day he left early and toward evening arrived in camp with two haunches and some other choice parts of a young cow moose. With fish and fresh meat available when needed, we did not, of course, anticipate any serious food shortage.

Cold rain fell off and on for three days, which had the merit of keeping our survivors in their bed rolls, gaining strength from moose broth, bolstered with a little finely chopped meat. It was not long before they were able to tolerate substantial meals of solid meat. During the intervals between rainfalls, Joe and I repaired the bady damaged canoe, using cedar strips, a sheet of birchbark, watap, and a mixture of seven parts of heated, dry jackpine resin and one part of fat. Now and then, the lads curiously peered out of the tent to see what we were about. They were personable young men, and both Joe and I came to admire their pluck and enjoy their congeniality. That they were able to carry on as long as they did, lost and with only a fish diet, finally without any food, was a credit to them.

As we sat around the evening campfires baking our bannock for the next day, I tried as tactfully as possible to learn how they had managed to wander back and forth over several routes so aimless and confused. They tried to link together the numerous segments of lake, river, and portage; but in their narration were apparently as confused as they had been in their actual disoriented canoe travels.

After five days the injured canoeist was able to hobble about on crutches made from the crotches of saplings. Approximately one hundred fifty miles of canoe and portage travel lay before us to the railroad. Our only problem now was in getting the injured lad over the portages. Although very slow, he did surprisingly well with his makeshift crutches, with frequent rests. His companion's only delegated task on the trip back was to watch him closely to prevent any misstep that could aggravate the break. Joe and I assumed the routine job of moving the canoes and packs over the portages and also, where necessary, carried the injured lad over the roughest terrain. For this we utilized the traditional method of making a stretcher simply by wrapping a folded tent floor-cloth between two forest-cut poles, held together by the weight of the one being carried. Where this was not practical on steeply sloped portages, Joe and I took turns carrying him piggyback.

Travel was delayed temporarily in order to keep the rendezvous with the Indians who had made the search toward the west. Since they did not wish to make the trip all the way to the railroad, I paid them for their services. They seemed very pleased to find the canoeists safe.

On the river route between the upper and lower lake regions, we met a very fine-looking Indian couple who were headed north to visit relatives. They had an eighteen-foot freighter canoe in excellent condition, good camp gear, and about a dozen recently shot ducks. The migration was on, ducks winging overhead at frequent intervals. We managed to hire this couple for the remaining part of the trip to the railhead, which helped considerably, of course, since the rescued canoeists, while recovering fairly well, had very little paddling strength or know-how when we got into rough water. The canoeists' damaged craft was abandoned, left a hundred feet back in the woods, to be salvaged later by the Indian couple for whatever use they could make of it.

A good tail wind, which sprang up on our arrival at the thirty-mile stretch of water to the south, prompted us to erect two so-called squaw sails, tent floor-cloths supported with two slim mast poles cut from the forest. Along with paddling, we covered the thirty miles in record time. Our Indian lady proved to be a very adept canoeist, willowy and strong.

Once we reached the railroad, we pitched our tents at the nearest waterfront to wait for the parents, whom we were able to contact after some delay, through the help of a railroad section-gang boss. It seemed wise to let the canoeists meet their parents in privacy. Therefore, when the train arrived, the Indians and I stayed out of sight at our camps on the waterfront until the family adjustment had been made. All of us finally met at our pitched camps where we had a feast, the parents having brought some luxury foods from Winnipeg.

The mothers of the canoeists took an immediate liking to

the attractive young Indian woman who had wielded a paddle so effectively over the last half of the recovery route back to the railroad. She and her husband were generously compensated for their assistance. I managed to acquire some items at the post to improve the splint dressing of the young man's fractured leg for travel to Winnipeg, where it could be put in a cast.

From the parents we learned that they had been back to the rail siding several times during the weeks of the search to make inquiries, and were beginning to have concern not only for their sons, but also for Joe and me. What had added to their worries was the possible hazard of illness by exposure because of the sudden drop in temperature from what it had been when their sons first started out on their trip. The only encouragement the parents had received over the period had come early from an Indian party reaching the railroad, who in the roundabout fashion of the grapevine, had learned that Joe and I were in the upper country continuing the search. But weeks had passed since that report.

Joe and I, extravagantly compensated, were now richer than we had ever been in our lives. On invitation of the parents and great insistence on the part of their sons, we accompanied them to Winnipeg, where we were, as the saying goes, treated royally. The young man's injured leg was immediately put in a cast, with crutches added for mobility. The doctor, clinically intrigued by my splinting job, took several pictures of it.

There seemed to be no end to the parents' generosity. Joe and I had purchased provisions, winter clothes, warmer sleeping equipment, guns, ammunition, tools, a roll of tar paper for a cabin roof, a stock item toboggan head, and other miscellaneous items, the cost of which added up to a substantial sum. As Joe and I were about to split the cost between us, the parents stepped in and insisted on defraying the entire expenditure.

Perhaps our protest was much too weak, or the bounds of their gratitude had become infinite.

Having crisscrossed the area where the canoeists had been, Joe and I decided to see and settle in a different part of the canoe country for the winter. Within the week, we were in a heavily loaded canoe at a takeoff point on the railroad, headed north through the Winnipeg, English, and Long-Legged rivers, to rough-in a temporary, cold weather cabin.

Joe has long since gone to the "Happy Hunting Ground." The parents of the canoeists, residents of the United States, passed away in the forties, as did one of the canoeists some ten years later. The last letter I was to receive from the second canoeist, in longhand, late in life, had an infirmity tremor in it due to age, or more likely an illness, which I had to consider significant. I did not see any of them, except Joe, after we parted in Winnipeg following the rescue. In memory, nevertheless, they are to me all still young, full of spirit, apprehension, generosity, and that priceless quality of human beings interacting with human beings for the good of all.

14

A Tragic Interlude

DOWN TOWARD THE BEGINNING of the century, I was enlisted by authorities to help bring out from the interior wilderness, by dogsled, a human body. Due to the strange circumstances surrounding the errand, I will withhold names and places.

Indians reaching the tiny wilderness settlements to sell some furs had reported the death of a white trapper, who, they said, had apparently died in bed, and judging from his reported age, death was presumed to have been from natural causes. One of the local Indians might have been enlisted to accompany the official, but I was fancy-free and welcomed any significant and worthwhile diversion from living alone in a cabin through the long northern winter. In youth, the winter trail does not seem arduous. If only it could continue that way throughout one's life!

Perhaps I felt much as my huskies did after weeks in their

chicken wire enclosures. They needed to flex their muscles, and so did I. When my dogsled was taken out of a cache building, drawn up over a mat of spruce boughs near the cabin to prevent the iced runners from freezing to the ground, my dogs were in a frenzy. They understood the purpose of such activity. They leaped at the chicken wire mesh, and the most eager of them tried to hurdle the high fence in frantic leaps, only to fall back floundering and disconsolate.

The start was to be early the next morning; in fact, well before dawn, since winter daylight in the North is short. I got to bed early, after a full day of food preparation: large pans of moose-meat stew were roasted in the oven, then removed to the outdoors where it was slush-frozen and finally frozen hard into separated, two-man, meal-size portions. I fried a generous number of doughnuts for the mug-ups (tea or coffee breaks) along the trail. Dog food was partially prepared to make cooking it on the trail an easier task—I used a dry oven process known to us in early days but since developed at great length for preparation of the "instant" foods.

Once during the night I awoke to hear a soughing sound, and saw wind-blown heavy snow scudding past the window. By morning the wind had reached gale proportions, and with a sudden radical drop in temperature to go with it, we had the two elements that constitute a blizzard, which hung on through the day. There was, of course, no great urgency to travel. The Indians, we learned, had seen to it that the dead trapper's cabin was well closed up; bears were in hibernation, and the likelihood of wolverines or other carnivores getting into the cabin to attack the body was quite remote.

By the second night the storm abated. Whereas I had awakened to see wind-driven snow the night before, I woke the second night to see moonlight filtering weakly through the heavily frosted window. Utter silence reigned. My watch showed 2 A.M. Rested beyond need because of the confining storm, I decided to stay up and make whatever adjustments were needed for an early start. Outdoors, the light from the nearly full moon bounced off the fresh white snow to light my every activity amply. The sled, having been covered with a tarp and lashed, was dug out of the snow and pulled up over a mat of newly cut boughs to free the runners. Snow was shoveled away from the cabin's entranceways and the routine snowshoe trails again broken and packed down to the outhouse, cache cabin, and water-supply hole in the ice.

The sled dogs, aware of my movements, had emerged from their individual houses in the chicken wire enclosure and were making enough noise to arouse people in the tiny wilderness settlement. I had scarcely completed my chores when my officer friend showed up, driving a dogsled to tote the body. I had agreed to drive a lighter sled to carry our gear and provisions. His dogs, of course, had answered mine, and apparently they had aroused him. With moonlight streaking across the snow-covered lake, he saw the merit of getting under way early to take advantage of the short northern daylight. There would be hard going in the soft, fresh snow, at least until subsequent winds had packed the snow on the lakes.

Travel began over the nearby lake ice which stretched for twenty-two miles haphazardly along coniferous forested shores, across multifingered bays that could confuse and frustrate travel if perchance we took the wrong bay to the river's mouth.

On snowshoes we took turns breaking trail ahead of the dogs—the unmanned team following close behind—and also alternated the lead positions of the two teams to give the dogs what relief we could afford them in the deep, soft snow.

Moving through the northern wilderness behind dog teams

"We took turns breaking trail . . ."

had for me in my early twenties a significance that only callow, aspiring youth can feel. To be traveling with an officer of the law at that age, despite my unofficial status, had me in a state of exuberance. I watched him as the apprentice watches the master. He could, I believed, do no wrong, and in observing his every movement, I looked for proper procedure.

Perhaps in my veneration, I overlooked the fact that my friend, though an officer of the law, was, like the rest of us, subject to the same frailties which make none of us human beings infallible. Naturally he tired, as did I, after long treks through the deep, soft snow. At times I thought he tired sooner than I, but then he was considerably older. No matter how weary, he never expressed it by complaint or irritation. In fact, I almost sensed his personal feelings were not allowed to be vented, lest he violate a code of being tolerant wherever tolerance paid off. Polite he was always, although when his politeness was practiced too diligently it seemed to become formality.

One might think that better than a formal politely impersonal approach for a person interacting with a companion on the wilderness trail would be to "act natural." But this, I hasten to say, often results in violent confrontation. Two men living the wilderness life closely too long can reach exasperation over the slightest difference between them concerning insignificant routine. Formality and self-restraint can thus save the day.

If during the entire journey I rationalized any of the foregoing, I am unable to recall at this time. The intervening years have been too many. I had, even at that early stage of my contact with the wilderness, critically examined with intense youthful ardor each aspect of camp equipment, and sedulously observed and practiced the methods of veterans who lived close to the wild. This might possibly have been manifest to the officer, for he accepted without question my camp and travel procedure, almost at times, I thought, allowing me generous leeway, while I carried out a share of the various camp and travel chores. He had an ingenious way of conveniently doing those things which did not occupy me. If I thoughtlessly usurped those tasks which might according to the circumstances have been attributed to his lot, he applied himself to other duties. Since that time, in my increasing years, I have interpreted this tolerance on his part as a wise general principle for one to practice in human relationship anywhere. His superiority in age and training had, no doubt, given him an advantage in understanding the impetuousness of youth, although I also would be inclined at this late moment to attribute our good relationship on the journey to my high respect for his official position, his exceptional skill in the wilderness—and perhaps more than these—to his continual integrity as a fine human being.

Our camps were made in the densest copses of spruce or balsam that we could find, in order to be well protected from the wind but always, as the officer put it, "near a wood pile." Fallen, dry timber had to be close enough at every camp to lessen the burdens of our task in creating a comfortable winter camp, although at times we supplemented the dry fuel with green birch, which burned after the fire had gotten well under way with dry wood. Camps, thus, were often in practical rather than picturesque surroundings. Fire-killed timber, when we found old burnings, provided fuel for some of our best open fires. At times we burned about a cord of such previously charred, handy, dry wood, there being, of course, no risk of forest fire in winter and no need for fuel economy. The big fires proved luxurious, their great heat radiation, felt even well away from the fire, allowing us to remove our parkas in sub-zero temperatures and no wind and move about almost as though we were in a heated room.

"I used the lean-to, reflecting type of tent with an open fire."

A Tragic Interlude

Winter camps of more recent years have seen the adoption of a double, wedge-type tent and a double-purpose stove, which can burn wood in the forest and be converted to burning oil on the arctic prairie. On the journey to bring out the trapper's body, and for several years thereafter, I used the lean-to, reflecting type of tent with an open fire. No doubt the closed wedge tent and stove provide a more adaptable combination, requiring much less fuel and affording simpler camp procedure. But there is something elementally outstanding in the open-front tent camp that lingers dramatically in retrospect. We capture a part of this effect before the open hearth fire in our homes. However, the imposing cold and the mystery of the surrounding forest need to be added. Perhaps we also require the fatigue of breaking trail all day through the snow to contrast with the haven of comfort we have provided in a winter wilderness.

How useless, actually, to attempt the analysis of the open fire: impalpable, mysterious, never dulling. It warms the body and elevates the spirit at the same time. When the darkness of night closes in, so do the doors of a camp close, by setting the vision limits a few feet beyond the fire's glow, simulating the coziness of the four walls of a more permanent abode.

After traversing numerous lakes and what in canoe travel season were portage trails, the officer and I finally came to the river mentioned by the Indians. At times we left the river and worked our way through dense undergrowth around ice hazards, to avoid the possibility of a breakthrough where in summer there were rapids or fast water. On several occasions we scaled rather steep inclines around waterfalls to get the sleds through portage trails, having to flounder in drifts without our snowshoes where they became only handicaps in the deep snow of the inclines. Here we gave the dogs help by preceding them with long trace lines as the dogs floundered in badly drifted hillside trails below us, moving as if swimming in the loose snow rather than treading upon solid footing. At other times we had to unhitch the dogs and bring them over the crest of the hillside, then run lines to the sleds, so that we and the dogs could get better footing to pull up the loads.

The cabin of the dead man had been described to us by the Indians as being on a small stream about five miles inland from the river. The deep snows could well disguise the mouth of the stream, but the Indians had considerately frozen an upright ten-foot spruce into the river ice near the stream's mouth, to identify the particular one of several streams flowing in from the west.

The final day's travel to the stream had been short, the previous camps so planned as to allow a few hours of daylight on reaching the cabin to investigate the possible cause of death, as the officer had suggested, even though the possibility of foul play, judging from the Indians' report, was believed to be remote. If we were to occupy the cabin for the night and could heat it, the frozen body would have to be left outdoors where it would be wrapped and lashed in a sled. After long, hard travel and camping out, we looked forward rather eagerly to the comfort of a heated cabin. These various points of convenience and method we had discussed at length in the previous night's camp.

Since I had been a medical corpsman in the Navy, we hoped that the first-aid training of the officer and the limited knowledge of disease I had gained through a war might enable us to determine the cause of the trapper's death, although this was highly speculative. The Indians' belief that it was of natural causes, a heart attack perhaps, suggested that the cause might be obscure to us, but would likely be a routine matter for medical men on the "outside" to diagnose, once we brought out the body.

A Tragic Interlude

About midafternoon we came upon the single spruce frozen into the river ice, and turned our course up the narrow stream. The prospect of not having to pitch a camp for the night made the remaining miles seem more easily traversed.

The cabin proved to be a low-roofed, rough type typically used by trappers, set in a small clearing. It was so well snowed in that the roof appeared to be resting on the snow. A long, shallow, untracked depression showed in the deep snow, no doubt made by the Indians' snowshoes before the last substantial snowfall. The officer studied the surrounding area, and concluded that the trapper had apparently been dead for some time. Freshly fallen snow does not completely obliterate signs of previous activity.

Using our snowshoes as shovels, we cleared the snow away from the entrance to the cabin and tramped down a snowshoe trail from our sleds to the four doghouses. This was a matter of routine examination through which deductions might be made by the officer as to what activity might have taken place around the premises. We looked into each doghouse, at the same time withdrawing from the snow the chains used to tether the animals. We feared finding the skeletal remains of four dogs, dead from starvation, but the chains held nothing at their snap ends. Obviously, the doghouses had previously been approached. We presumed that the Indians, on finding the trapper dead, had released the dogs to forage for themselves. At least, we concluded, mercy had been shown here by somebody. Later information revealed that neither had the Indians found dogs tethered when they stopped at the cabin to check on the trapper's welfare. Had the trapper, expecting to die, released the dogs himself?

The officer pushed open the door to the cabin and entered. I followed close on his heels. He stopped just inside the door, surveying everything in sight, then walked over to the rude bed constructed of forest-cut poles, mattressed with balsam boughs, and peered down on the uncovered face of the corpse. He was about to lift a rabbit-skin robe and some Hudson's Bay blankets off the corpse when we noticed something in the facial tissues that made us pause. My medical corps training was sufficient to tell me that the pustular eruption and febrile aspect of the corpse's skin, even though frozen hard, were probably symptoms of smallpox.

What initially had seemed a routine matter of bringing out a body now loomed up as a possible clinical investigation of all Indians trapping in the general area. One of the most contagious diseases might be running rampant. And yet, our limited knowledge of the symptoms of the disease was too meager to give this whole matter a final resolution. Medical officialdom would likely have to make the best disposition of the matter. To haul out the body might spread the disease; we did not know. We were not even sure that we ourselves had not already become infected and would spread the disease to Indians in the region if we reconnoitered to find any possible similar cases. We consoled ourselves with the fact that both of us had been vaccinated. The trail to this cabin from the outside medical world was long, cold, and difficult. How should disposition be made?

We closed the cabin and drove our teams a quarter mile upstream, where we set up our camp. There was a large, wood-burning, airtight stove in the cabin, but our best judgment told us to leave everything in the cabin frozen solid. In our tent camp that night we discussed every possibility. If the body were not brought out, the medical authorities would not know whether it actually was a case of smallpox. We would have to provide them with whatever we could for their diagnosis.

A Tragic Interlude

The following day we returned to the cabin, where we found some screw-top receptacles which we sterilized by boiling them in one of the trapper's cooking utensils over an open outdoor fire. We then took skin tissue and smears which we thought could be used for diagnosis, taking every precaution to avoid possible contagion. The body was otherwise left as it was found, the cabin sealed up and posted for quarantine.

What the disposition eventually was, I did not learn. I was asked not to mention the matter in the tiny settlement, presumably to avoid risking panic among people who might fear an epidemic even where contagion might not have existed.

Some years later I had occasion to travel through the region by canoe with an Indian friend of mine. He has long since gone over that divide from which there is no returning, so will never know why I stopped at a certain point on the river where we camped, and made my way alone on foot five miles along a narrow stream, through dense tag alders, to a certain trapper's cabin site. The effect of an early clearing was there, but heavily overgrown with brush. Where the cabin had been stood a rusted-out stove. Fifty feet back in the forest, almost obscured by vegetation, was a mound of soil which might have been a grave. I made no inquiries and drew no conclusions.

15

Prospector Prospecting for a Wife

THE CANADIAN NATIONAL, a transcontinental train on which I was traveling, came to a screeching stop in the dark of a rain-drenched night in the Ontario forest where a trestle spanned a river. I doubt that today's scheduling, in the grasp of railroad officialdom with demands for exacting revenue, would permit such a wilderness stop.

It did, with a high average of accommodation, earlier in the century. I was trying to reach a prospector friend of mine who had roughed out a temporary log cabin at the confluence of four streams that finally merged into a single one, subsequently to find its way into the Albany River. As all roads lead to Rome, it became apparent that where rivers were concerned, a surprising number—the Pagwachuan, Kenogami, Nagagami, Kabinakagami, and others—led to my friend's cabin.

The peculiar directions for finding his cabin, which months earlier he had supplied in a letter to me, included elements of both amusement and adventure: "If in the night the engineer misses a river trestle crossing, try to get a stop at the next river trestle crossing. Any of these crossings are only about fifty miles by river from my cabin. The water will be high when you get here, so you won't be too long on the downstream trip."

Rain was falling heavily when the train crew deposited me in the night at the river crossing. I could not even see the river below with the aid of a flashlight. Rain being as normal as sunshine in the Ontario wilderness, however, I was prepared for it. Dressed in a rain shirt, a sou'wester (the wide-brimmed rain hat), and a pair of lightweight, four-buckle overshoes, I would remain fairly dry, come what may. My two Poirer packs, one loaded with provisions, the other with camp gear, were as rainproof as I was—waterproof bag liners within guarding all, proof from wetting even in the event of a canoe upset.

I found a pile of bridge-repair timbers where I could invert the canoe, prop up one end to get under it, and avoid the annoyance of rain and hail pounding down on me. Seated there on a projecting timber in the pile, I half dozed on and off until daylight.

With the first glimmer of dawn I saw the river below and made ready to get under way, to travel at least far enough downstream to find a spot where I could pitch a tent, raise half of it as a canopy, and build a fire under it to prepare my breakfast. If possible, I wanted to get far enough from the railroad train noises in this first camp to enjoy the peace of the northern wilds. I later found that the low rumble of trains, especially long freights, crossing the trestle broke the silence a surprising number of miles away. Once the trains were gone the silence seemed even deeper and more comforting.

As I swung close to one bank in my canoe, I noticed something dangling from the tip of a dead cedar that projected well out over the stream—such trees commonly referred to as "sweepers." The dangling object turned out to be a pair of worn-out, moosehide, wrap-around Indian moccasins that had been patched and re-patched, obviously tied there to designate a small Indian camp area upon the immediate river bank. On landing I found tent poles and stakes handily leaning up against a tree. A few blackened stones, apparently used for cooking pail props, showed where there had been previous campfires.

Relieved to get out of my rain gear after collecting some firewood, I quickly erected my tent. One suffers a certain amount of condensation moisture in undergarments when wearing rain gear even though it sheds the downpour. Just beyond the tent canopy, I built a substantial drying fire, big enough to resist being dampened by the rain, which by this time had settled down to a light, steady drizzle. The fire going well, I was able to rake aside some glowing embers for making a breakfast of pancakes, ham, coffee, and dried apricots.

The weather was mild enough, but having spent half a night under a canoe in a driving rain, I needed a certain amount of thawing out. The fire soon burned down to a glowing bed and needed only small amounts of wood at intervals to continue the drying process.

Losing sleep is something I have never been able to do gracefully. In anticipation of getting that train to stop at one of the river trestle crossings, I had kept wide awake to continually ride herd on the train crew, so that they wouldn't forget my departure point. They had it fully in mind. In fact, as I learned, they had discussed among themselves the advisability of their passenger's being "dumped out in the Ontario wilderness in the rain and hail," but had agreed that he was "young and tough and seems to know what the hell he is doing." The brakeman, offering encouragement, had muttered close to my ear, "I hope to Christ you make it, brother." I thought about this as I stretched out comfortably on a down robe before the fire. Although I appreciated the compassionate attitude of the train crew, I was a bit perplexed that people should look so disconcertedly upon the wilderness, when actually coping with the situation confronting me that night required no particular extension of effort.

How long I had dozed into the day, I did not know; but suddenly awake, I saw a large, well-built Indian in a buckskin shirt and mackinaw pants looking down on me from a short distance away, with a smile that seemed to light up the whole outdoors. He had as perfect a set of teeth as I have ever seen. Behind him, seated in a birchbark canoe at the water's edge, was a young woman, and propped up against a thwart was a *tikinakun* (cradle board), holding an unusually cute, round-faced baby. Despite the man's amiable smile, there seemed to be concern written on his face. He and his family had intended to camp on the spot for the night; seeing the well-known place occupied, they would have gone on, except that first finding no one stirring about the camp and then finding a man lying in his tent in the daytime suggested possible illness or injury.

His fears of my being ill and his concern about intrusion allayed, we soon were sitting around the fire eating his venison and my bannocks, along with the remaining stewed apricots I had prepared earlier. I put some powdered whole milk in a shaker can, added enough water to re-constitute what might be considered a standard milk, and handed it to the mother, pointing toward the baby. It brought a smile of approval. She finally drank it, since the baby apparently had a better source of supply.

The couple was headed toward the interior to visit with relatives. They knew where the rough little cabin of my prospector friend was located, were acquainted with him, and would be glad, they said, to have me travel with them to his place, from which point they would continue on. While it seemed apparent that I should have no trouble reaching the confluence of the rivers and finding the cabin on my own, traveling with this family did greatly simplify matters, as well as heighten my pleasure and knowledge of Indian life.

The mother spoke little, even to her husband in the Cree tongue. The baby, a boy, must have inherited the father's captivating smile, because whenever the baby smiled, his face was the image of his father's and had us all in a gleeful mood. They continued to politely hesitate a little about pitching their tent in the same area as mine, but I managed with little trouble to overcome their reluctance by moving my small tent to a secluded spot nearby on the river, so that they could have the immediate, long-used area in private.

On a number of occasions over my years of wilderness travel, I have had the fortunate circumstance of coming onto overnight Indian camps, or Indians have come onto my camps. The first such contacts pose a moment of embarrassment; however, this I have found easy to overcome, and some of my richest associations with Indians have resulted from these coincidental meetings.

The sky cleared toward evening, the river reflecting the orange glow of a magnificent sunset. I was "slept out" and content to sit by the river's edge and listen to the night sounds of the forest. I do not know what time it was when I again became drowsy; but I quietly slipped into my down sleeping robe, lay there listening to further sounds of the forest, and soon fell asleep. When I awoke at the first glow of dawn, the Indian family already had a fire going to prepare our breakfast. The fire felt good that early in the morning. The sky was clear, and I looked forward to a promising day for heading down the river.

It was the Indians who knew most about the wilderness to the north in that early period. The river that seemed to be a kind of Ultima Thule to this Indian family was Ontario's great Severn, which starts in the vast lake region at about West Longitude 95° and North Latitude 53°, then divides into a double river one hundred fifty miles to the east, where its earlier double flow joins as one stream, and continues about two hundred miles more to Hudson Bay. There, the Indian family said they had relatives who trapped.

Traveling leisurely, in fact dallying and largely floating downstream, we camped again before reaching the temporary cabin of my prospector friend. On my arrival at the cabin, I found that he had left a week earlier. On the table was a note which read:

Cal, make yourself at home. I've gone to Winnipeg to see if I can find a girl to marry. There is plenty of grub up in the meat cache. Don't fall off the ladder. Have struck it pretty good in my prospecting off to the east, and can now support a wife if she doesn't have too high-toned ideas. The trouble is, will she take to the bush with me for a few more years of prospecting. I'll be back as soon as I can find what I'm looking for. See you in about two weeks. I have built a new, peeled log cabin west of Nipigon. Wish me luck. I need a woman.

The present so-called "log shack" was a better product than his derogatory remarks regarding it in his correspondence had suggested. The logs still had the bark on them, and the floor was made from only roughly flattened poles; but all was neat and cozy. A small shelf of books promised some leisurely hours of reading until his return. However, the surrounding wilderness held for me a greater attraction.

Reading the note of my prospector friend's matrimonial aspirations immediately brought to mind an unusual meeting I had had on the Canadian National train shortly after boarding it at Winnipeg. Traveling first-class was an attractive young white woman, possibly twenty-six years of age, dressed in buckskin. The garments were of Indian-tanned skins and unusual cut. While not actually soiled, they did, nevertheless, show some effects of wear. Had the garments been immaculately clean and commercially tanned, I would have presumed that she possibly was a circus performer, or merely an individual with a flare for exotic dress. Obviously, the buckskin suit had been worn outdoors in some active pursuit, for it conformed well to her body.

Naturally, my curiosity about her was aroused. Where would a young, attractive woman, dressed in a rather rough and ready buckskin suit, be heading, riding first-class on a transcontinental train? On the other hand, perhaps she might have asked herself about me, "Where is a young man heading, riding first-class, dressed in bush clothes?"

When I discreetly asked the conductor about her, his answer was gruffly to the point: "Why don't you ask *her?*"

I thought so personal a query too presumptuous and hoped for a genial glance from her that might enable me to make the obtrusion. Later when I entered the diner, she was seated alone at a table. Whether there had been collusion here by the train crew, I do not know, but I was brought to her table, ostensibly to use the tables most conveniently. She was at once agreeable to my sharing the table.

She opened the conversation. I qualified my bush dress; she qualified hers. Her husband, now deceased, had been employed by eastern mining interests, and having done quite well, had given up his employment to go into freelance prospecting. Together, she and her husband had staked out some claims, had built a temporary cabin in a promising area, and were busy prospecting and test-drilling when her husband had a fatal heart attack. Earlier, a kerosene mantle lamp had, by building up soot, overheated the font and exploded in the cabin, and despite their efforts to extinguish the flames, they had lost the cabin and nearly all of their equipment, including their clothes —thus the well-worn buckskin suit. The young widow believed that it was the desperate effort to save their equipment, the cabin, and to prevent a forest fire, that had brought on her late husband's fatal heart attack. She was now returning from Winnipeg where she had gone to get some claim-developing help, but where she had found that the only speculation money offered was on a basis of the mining companies' acquiring the mineral rights and getting the lion's share if the claims proved out.

She asked me if I would be willing to help her buy some equipment and go back to the claims. A very capable Indian who she called "Soomy" had worked with her husband, and she said he would help us build a new cabin.

She was convincing. I had various suspicions of being conned, but suppressed them. As the train raced around curves that skirted lake shores, rumbled over the trestles spanning rivers, even seemed to cleave masses of Precambrian rock in the cuts, my mind was doing fantastic curves, spannings, and cleavages of its own. Suppose that I chose not to get dumped into the driving rain and dark at the trestle, but went on with her to the east: what would lie in wait?

She was no ordinary woman. In the dining car, she was concerned about my dinner, saying, "You had better eat. No telling how soon you will get another good meal out there in the rain." The advice had the earmarks of wilderness experience. She herself ate sparingly, even though I had made it clear that she was my dinner guest. "I'll be sitting around," she explained, "and one doesn't need much food for that." My suspicions of being conned diminished somewhat.

I had been jumping to conclusions in several respects. I considered she might be down on her luck in more ways than having lost her husband, until she told me that she had ample income. When she had asked if I would be willing to buy some equipment, I naturally presumed that what she needed was someone to finance and assist her in another prospecting operation. It became clear as the discussion went along that above all else she needed someone who knew the bush and could cope with it. She was even willing to bear the initial expense, if necessary, and to share the proceeds. Instinctively, I recognized that she needed more than this.

Romance? I broached the subject. "If you are afraid of me," she smiled, "you can stay in Soomy's cabin." Well. Maybe. I knew better. When she told me that I could drop her at the first railroad stop if the claims proved up or failed, we ceased talking about inevitable sexual involvement. In my diary I wrote down her name and address, noted where she might be from time to time, and even added a few names of her friends, who would know her whereabouts. I would visit my friend up at the confluence of the rivers, I told her, and then get in touch. At least, I toyed with the idea. That my friend was looking for a wife, I had not, of course, learned as yet; therefore, I had no particular reason to discuss him with her, except to mention that he was a good friend. I was thinking more of the option that was open for me should I later decide to pick it up.

We had visited until I was ready to disembark with my packs

and canoe at the trestle. Standing on the coach step, she offered words of encouragement, disregarding the rain which was hitting her in the face.

As I now studied the prospector's note, I turned a half dozen ideas over in my mind as possibilities. Suppose I sent a letter to the girl in buckskin and told her that my prospector friend was looking for a wife, only to find that he had already mustered one from the ranks of Winnipeg women. If he did not return very soon and had no success, would the girl in buckskin by that time have made other plans? If my prospector friend was not willing to throw in with a woman partner where there might be no further relationship, what then? Would I be playing both cupid and entrepreneur, only to find that I had meddled where I should have minded my own business? I meddled.

Because of my remote situation, I couldn't do anything immediately. However, several days later a small party of Indians heading for the railroad came by, and I saw an opportunity. They accepted my invitation to stop for lunch and tea, while I got off two communications, one for the girl in buckskin and the other to the Empire Hotel in Winnipeg, where the prospector usually stayed when in that city. In the letter to him, I gave a brief about the girl in buckskin; and in the letter to her, I quoted the note I had before me in the cabin. The Indians promised to get the letters into the hands of the railroad section gang for mailing.

By getting the messages off this soon, I felt that I had caught a timely opportunity, and although I had some apprehensions about the possible consequences of playing cupid, I dismissed the whole affair for the time being, and began to enjoy my lone visit in the surrounding country. Whenever I took off for a day or two of exploring around and camping out, I left a note in the cabin, indicating the general area where I might be and when I would be back at the cabin.

It was on the return from such an overnight camping trip that I saw smoke coming from the chimney of the prospector's cabin. I found that he had returned and was alone.

We had not seen each other for some time, and while both of us finally had much to say about his matrimonial aspirations, at first we talked principally about our respective lives, filling in the blanks for the time that had lapsed since our last visit.

Finally, I asked, "What about your prospecting for a beauteous maiden? Couldn't you talk one into marrying you?"

His answer was astonishing. "Offer them marriage," he said, "and you can have anyone you want."

He was what one might call a ruggedly handsome man, in his mid-thirties. We had on one occasion spent some time together in Winnipeg, after having been in the wilderness on a canoe journey. I had the impression that women were attracted to him. His wit and apparent charisma seemed to charm them. The stories he told me about his prospecting for a wife in Winnipeg could in themselves make a book. It might be said that he covered the waterfront. In one instance, he amusingly explained that this was literal, since he had managed through a friend to spend some time at a fashionable boat club, where women in their bathing suits were "more like mermaids," he reflected, "their physical assets revealed." The closest he came to finding someone who might brave the bush was an attractive farm girl who had ventured into the big city to increase her chances of getting the "right kind of husband." Apparently she had assayed her feminine advantages. She was employed as a waitress in a first-class restaurant.

"I had her out a few times," he said, "and I have her address. I liked her. She didn't know that I was in Winnipeg looking for a wife. She was glad to leave the farm, so I don't know if she would work out roughing it in the bush for a few years. She was a charmer for looks."

Then came the bombshell. How he had so casually held off exploding it much earlier, I am still amazed. With a mischievous, triumphant smile, he said, "I got your letter at the Empire Hotel and called your friend in buckskin on the phone. I was two days in getting in touch with her."

"Well, what happened?" I anxiously interjected.

"She's coming here. She is willing to go it on a straight business deal. If we can hit it off as man and wife, that will have to be seen. If we don't like what we find in each other, we part as friends. On this we agreed. I told her that was pretty cold, but she seemed willing to have it that way unless our impressions decided something else. Women are clever as hell, you know."

We talked far into the night, making coffee about every two hours. Off and on, the big question from him was, "What exactly is she like?"

"Much too attractive to bloom and blush unseen here in the bush," I chided him.

I had no intention of building her up beyond my best appraisal from the short acquaintance. What seemed to appeal to him in my description, besides her physical charm, was that she appeared to be intelligent, compassionate, and considerate. That she responded so well to wilderness life seemed to resolve his biggest problem. He liked the impression I had imparted to him of her standing on the lower step of the train, giving me encouragement while she endured, without flinching, the rain and hail beating at her.

"I believe a man could make it with a woman like that," he said, "but we will have to see."

That she was willing, as he put it, "to return to the diggins" after she lost her husband, and not abandon the project for an easier life, gave him the additional support he needed.

With some cooperation from the section gang, he was to pick up the lady in buckskin at a small station, the two of them then to be taken by handcar, the so-called "go-devil," to the trestle where it crossed the river. My prospector friend had told her in his phone conversation that he wanted to see her arrive in the buckskin suit, since I had verbally sketched the picture of her so dressed. I remained back at the river with the canoe, allowing him to meet her alone. About two hours later I heard the handcar rattle along the track and come to rest at the trestle. I had tea and lunch ready by the time they joined me at the river's edge.

If a study of facial expressions and gestures reveals anything, I saw the glow of happiness in a couple who were to succeed in a mining operation and no less matrimonially. A month later they were married in Winnipeg. I was to visit them several times over the years. She always derived great amusement by telling people in my presence that I was the only man who had ever "jilted" her.

16

The Sourdough Legend

IF YOU BELONG to that legion who traverse the wilderness at length, your ears should prick up at the sound of the word "sourdough." This pertains no matter what your mode of wilderness travel, be it packhorse, canoe, dogsled, snowmobile, or on foot. The reason will become patent on the barest examination. Since the use of sourdough applies as much in modern-day wilderness living as it did in generations past, we might best consider the essential need for it in the wilds, and why it has become a tradition, if not a dire necessity.

Where the ingredients of sourdough are not known or not understood, travel in the wilderness includes bread in the provisions about as follows: only enough fresh yeast-leavened bread packed at the start of the trip to last until it becomes stale. Breads used from then on are usually made with baking powder as the leavening agent, or unleavened breads are carried, such as hardtack, sea biscuits, soda crackers, and the like. As a steady diet these cracker-type breads have two faults: they are not substantial enough as a full complement to other foods; and most of them, not being yeast bread, affect the digestive system in the same manner as baking powder and soda-leavened breads, creating biliousness which in time, if the trip is of long duration, can become so acute as to give one continual gastric distress throughout the trip.

This problem has been for centuries and is today resolved in the wilderness by the sourdough method of baking bannock, biscuits, flapjacks, dumplings, or whatever is made from flour and requires leavening.

Earlier, in the wilderness cabin, in a warm but not hot place near the stove on a shelf, there stood an earthenware crock of sourdough with a loose-fitting wooden cover. If you removed the cover you would likely find around the inside wall of the crock a thick incrustation that resembled a giant-sized corncob pipe. You could conclude from this incrustation that the batch— referred to by the long-established vernacular term "starter"— was *started* a long time ago. Perhaps a small amount had been carried over from the "Old Country" during the early fur trade or the colonizing period and had been kept fermenting ever since by the simple, periodic replenishment of nothing more than flour and water.

When the wooden cover was removed from the sourdough crock, it emitted an odor like a Kentucky mountain still. If you stayed for breakfast, very probably you would be served flapjacks leavened and flavored with this sourdough, which did not in the end product taste or smell at all like the starter itself. The miracle of this lay in the fact that chemically the acid nature of the starter was altered in the recipe by the addition of an alkali, consisting of either soda or baking powder; and inversely, the soda or baking powder, it can be said, chemically altered the acid sourdough. When the flapjack batter hit the hot griddle, the resulting gas which formed rose in numerous bubbles to the top of the flapjack, making the cakes light.

As mentioned, long use of only soda or baking powder as a leavening agent in breads can cause a digestive disorder. When these alkaline ingredients are neutralized by the acid of the sourdough, their bad effects no longer obtain. In fact, what we have in the baked end product is something that seems to aid rather than hinder digestion. As a trapper once told me, and I believe with some merit, "You will never get a bellyache from sourdough, and if you have a bellyache it will damn well cure it."

We need especially to bear in mind that sourdough is not only a leavening agent but, as previously indicated, a very effective flavoring agent as well. A firm on the West Coast is now making seventy-five thousand loaves of sourdough bread daily, and this industry promises to spread. Common loaf bread and biscuits get their leavening and flavor basically in the same way but in greatly modified form, by using the leavening agent of yeast. The underlying difference is that in sourdough the microorganisms are allowed to develop far more abundantly than in common yeast—the intentional prolonging of the fermentation period results in an increase in microorganisms, thereby enhancing the special flavor of sourdough breads. The final recipe in which sourdough is used has something to do, of course, with the various caprices of flavor. Buckwheat flapjacks may, for example, please one taste while straight wheat cakes may appeal to another. Sourdough does, nevertheless, improve them all.

We thus have a bread for the trail in the sourdough process that can be eaten in abundance with no ill effects. From clinical analysis now going on at various universities concerning the effect of the sourdough microorganism on the digestive system, there seems to be concurrence in the idea that we have something valuable here.

The backwoods notions regarding sourdough have built up some strange legends about origins of starters. Many of them continue to be veiled in secrecy. The sourdough starters brought over from Europe and spread throughout Canada and the United States as legendary formulas, fermenting, as we might say, "in perpetuity," were purported to have a particular microorganism which could not be developed by anybody "from scratch." I have no desire to discredit these theories. Tastes differ and sentiment is as significant in legends as in caprice of appetite. If the starters serve the epicurean tradition, or even delusion, by all means let us encourage their continuance. We often see the various effects of psychology on the taste of food.

The latest trouble with the sourdough secret mixture theory is that a "snoopy bunch of scientists" have been peering into the trapper's sourdough crock and have pulled the curtain away from the early illusion of magic. Some of these early mixtures brought from Europe got their fermentation from hops and other substances, others from buttermilk, and still others from only a tablespoon of vinegar added to the flour and water, or merely from the simple mixture of flour and water allowed to sour.

In the evolutionary order of sourdough starters, the incipient mixture was, no doubt, just flour and water allowed to ferment; next, flour, water, and a tablespoonful of sugar, the addition of sugar speeding up the fermentation; then flour, water, sugar, and yeast; and finally, flour, water, sugar, yeast, and lactic acid—the latter in the form of buttermilk. It is this last formula which has proven the most outstandingly good and flavorful sourdough starter—the one which has been enhanced by scientific effort and is now generally most approved.

No salt is added to the basic starter. Salt inhibits fermentation. Salt will, however, have to be added to the final recipe in which sourdough is used.

The method of making a sourdough starter is rather simple. An average batch is made as follows: A gallon-size earthenware crock or glass jar is needed, with either a wooden cover or a porcelain plate for a cover. Pour about three pints of warm (not hot) water and a cup of buttermilk into the crock or jar. Dissolve a cake of yeast or a small envelope of dry yeast separately in a half cup of warm (not hot) water, and add this to the liquid mixture. Stir in about two tablespoonfuls of sugar. All of these amounts can be approximate. Finally, stir in enough sifted flour to bring it to about the consistency of pancake batter; mix thoroughly. Let this mixture ferment at room temperature for at least three days before use. It will develop a watery liquid on top. Before using, stir this liquid back into the batter to get a smooth blend, but do not beat it, as this would release too much of the leavening gas and weaken the starter for a day or so.

To make bread, bannock, biscuits, flapjacks, dumplings, and the like, one simply follows the recipe in any cookbook, except to leave out the leavening agent called for in the cookbook and substitute the following: a cup of sourdough starter to which has been added one-half teaspoon or less of baking soda or half the baking powder called for in the recipe. It will be found that baking powder is superior to soda, since it adds something extra to the leavening process; otherwise, baking powder performs the same function and does not impart the characteristic taste that occurs if too much soda is used. As to the size of the batch, your cup of sourdough will constitute about half the liquid in your recipe.

This is the point where one becomes the expert or the dunce

in the sourdough cooking class. Sourdough varies in strength from age and temperature, so that a happy balance has to be reached in the amount of baking powder or soda that is added to the cup of starter. It is better to err by putting either *too little soda* or *too much baking powder* into the mixture. Experiment with small batches until you get the best leavening and taste.

On removing a cup of sourdough from the starter for baking, replenish the starter with only flour and water. Now and then, if the starter seems a bit weak, activate it by adding a cup of buttermilk.

On the trail you will have to use a sourdough pail instead of a crock, to avoid breakage and provide convenience in carrying. If you can pick up from your camp equipment supplier a stainless steel pail with a cover and a bail, or arched handle, you will be best off. The acid sourdough tends to attack the metal of aluminum or lightly plated steel vessels. It helps to line them with a film of beeswax, heating the beeswax in the vessel and pouring out the excess. The container can also be made square, of wood with a wire or wood bail and a wood cover. The cover should be recessed to hold it in place. The wood joints in the container should be good. A receptacle can also be made of birchbark. All covers must fit loosely enough to allow the fermentation gas to escape; otherwise the cover might pop off from built-up pressure. On the trail, carry the sourdough container in hand by the bail. Some campers bury the sourdough pail in the flour sack, others fix it securely in a grub box—always set upright, of course. All except the hand-carrying method seem to prove failures. On portage trails it is well to set the container down in a conspicuous place where it won't be forgotten—yet not be kicked over. On a packhorse trip the sourdough container should be placed at the bottom of a pannier, after first having been put in a rubberized, waterproof bag, in the event that the pack animal should take a roll or a fall.

Sourdough biscuits and sourdough dumplings are most traditional in the prairie and desert cattle country, while the bannock has its traditional place in the northern wilderness. But I hasten to add that sourdough is universal. And the best way to become an expert at it is to begin with a crock at home, wherever you are, and build up a background sourdough knowledge that will fit the wilderness. Trail methods of baking sourdough breadstuffs vary according to the mode of travel and the kind of baking utensils practicable in the country.

The sixteen-quart Dutch oven, the kettle-like, cast-iron vessel shown in the illustration, with legs and a rimmed cover along with a bail, is the item integral to the cooking procedures of the chuck wagon as well as the packhorse train. Inside the Dutch oven is a trivet—a round, flat iron plate with numerous heat vent-holes which also serve to lighten it, and short legs or bosses that keep it off the bottom of the oven. To bake a pan of biscuits, place the raw biscuits in a low-sided cake pan and set it in the oven on the trivet. Because the pan is kept off the bottom by the trivet there is uniform heat all around. While you have been preparing the biscuits for baking, a fire made from piñon pine, mesquite, greasewood, or other fuels, if you are in the Southwest, and other fuels native to the area elsewhere, will have been burning down to a bed of glowing coals. The Dutch oven will be set on the coals, with a small amount of the coals piled on the cover—the high rim mentioned retaining them and their heat for baking the biscuits on top as well. Experience alone will soon tell how many of the hot coals are needed proportionately on top and bottom.

The cast-iron Dutch oven is truly an extraordinary device, and

The Dutch oven—a truly convenient device.

I would carry it on more than packhorse trips if it were not so heavy. However, an aluminum Dutch oven is now on the market which is one-third the weight of the steel oven but identical in shape, and is made in two sizes, twelve-inch and ten-inch diameter. It might be a temptation to take one of these along, even on a canoe trip. It could have other general use, such as in heating water and cooking large amounts of meat and fish to preserve them for later consumption, replacing the largest pail in the regular cook kit, thus compensating somewhat for the weight of the Dutch oven.

For canoe trips you may want a folding aluminum reflector oven for baking your biscuits. The illustration here shows the method. You do not want glowing coals but a flashing flame that flares well above the top height of your reflector and about eight inches away. The trick is to keep the flames high enough so that the top as well as the bottom of your bread or biscuits gets uniformly baked by reflection. If too much heat builds up at the bottom because a burned-down bed of coals has accumulated, stick a small piece of green wood between the fire and the bottom front half of the oven during part of the baking period. Preferably, a flat piece of aluminum can be hung on the baking pan in such a way as to shut off some of the heat from the bottom of the pan when necessary.

If you have considerable woodland experience, you will probably omit the reflector oven and get down to the simpler method of baking bannock in a steep-sided, long-handled frying pan, as shown in the accompanying illustration. Bake the top side of the bannock by reflection, then flip the bannock over and bake the bottom the same way. Or, bake the bottom first by holding the pan well above the flame, then bake the top by propping the pan up before the fire. You will likely burn the bottom of the bannock on your initial try, so keep the pan safely above the

The reflector oven method

The bannock pan method

flames and be patient. Don't grill the bannock quickly like a pancake; slowly bake it.

Some bannock bakers build a fire on a flat piece of ground, let the fire burn down to a bed of coals, scrape the coals away, set the fry pan with the bannock on the bare hot ground, cover the pan with a piece of tin with turned-up edges, place hot coals on the tin, and let the bannock bake until brown, top and bottom. The baking dough can be inspected from time to time by lifting the tin with a pair of pliers or a pot holder. However, for convenience I think you will prefer the reflecting method.

In either the reflector oven or the bannock pan type of baking, where only reflected flames are used, keep the breadstuffs as mentioned about eight inches from the fire, but you can vary the distance according to the intensity of the flames. In the Arctic, where you use only a Primus stove, keep the bannock very thin and cook it like a pancake, though more slowly.

Sourdough bread doughs will rise both before and as they bake. If you want extra-light breads and have the time, allow whatever degree of rising you prefer by keeping the dough in a warm (not hot) place before baking. If the bannock or biscuits are not made to rise before baking, keep them thin in the baking pan, and give them a rich brown crust.

The appellation "sourdough," as applied to a woodsman, has become common terminology. Perhaps it is now gaining more of a generic connotation; however, I think we can trace its origin to a designation for the early prospectors and miners along the creeks of Alaska and the Yukon Territory, no self-respecting one of whom would have been caught without a sourdough crock in his cabin. There were, no doubt, good camp cooks around, but the real test of a wilderness sojourner was whether he could come up with a tasty sourdough bannock, varied from plain bread to fancy coffee cake. The main reason for this test was that whoever lived much off the land on a meat diet needed something to go with the meat and give gastronomic interest to the trailside mug-up. Potatoes were not carried. Bannock was the best substitute. Today, of course, we have instant potatoes, instant rice, and other such foods to complement our diet of meat. Yet we may ask, what takes the place of hot bread, browned to a T, with slathers of butter, or peanut butter and jam? Enriched with ingredients for a coffee cake, it can make a rainy day as pleasurable as sunshine.

17

The Wilderness Indigene

THERE COMES A TIME in our lives when a personal decision is made as to where we should settle as permanent residents—and particularly about what are our most environmentally desirable choices. I suppose the alternative to permanent residence is to become peripatetic and consider the whole world one's living province. But that choice proves finally to weary. There is something culturally fascinating and romantic about having been born and lived one's entire life in a certain region. We often boast of being indigenous products of a place, no matter how well traveled we are. In Labrador the indigene is referred to as the "liveyere" (live here)—the person who was born and raised on the Labrador coast, not the transient or anyone who by some circumstance came to take up life in that area.

When we consider the indigene as he relates to wilderness, we become involved in a great complexity of species adaptation, of natural selection, and other processes—scientific speculations beyond the scope of this chapter or book. Rather, what might seem of significance here is the average degree of human adjustment to various natural areas.

It is not strange, for example, that a certain Texan reviewing one of my recent books, *Once Upon a Wilderness,* took offense at my not having given quite as much emphasis to the prairie as I had to other natural areas. Having earlier in life spent two years on the wilderness prairie myself, I can identify in part with the reviewer, and see him mounting a horse to ride out into free, open spaces, with no particular wish to forgo his ride over the plains for wilderness travel through dense forest, lakes, or even moutain terrain. A prairie rancher once told me that he suffered a claustrophobic feeling when he was in the "confines of the forest."

Compare this feeling with that of the Quebec woodsman who took a recreational train ride to the west coast of Canada, and remarked about the Canadian prairies that for a whole day the train traveled "through space where there was nothing." Or, what about the newlyweds who left a metropolis and went to one of the most spectacular, scenic, mountain resort areas on the continent, where—wholly oblivious to the grandeur and multiplicity of natural subjects to engage their interest—they complained to the management a few hours after arriving, "What are we supposed to do here, just look at the scenery?"

Stewart Edward White, whose books on the wilderness were current near the beginning of this century, divided most of his outdoor literary interest between the north lake country and the western mountains, although he did some writing on other regions. One of the observations he made was that the mountains did not give him the intimacy which he found in the lesser elevations of the Precambrian shield region of lakes, rivers, and forests.

I mentioned this to a friend whose focus as he approached retirement was to build a cabin in the mountains. "It's the majesty of the mountains," he said, "that gives me the greatest wilderness inspiration." And added, "When a mountain stream tumbles past my door, coming from the snows on the peaks, I know it's the purest water in the world, and has the finest fish."

Years passed following that conversation. One day a letter came inviting me to spend some time with him—as he put it, "in the most intimate little cabin, in the most majestic mountains on the continent." I wondered how Stewart Edward White would have responded to that viewpoint, contradictory by his definition.

I rode all day on the desert to get to my friend's mountain cabin, while just ahead of me plodded a burro with my camp equipment and provisions. I was tired and dehydrated toward the end of the day. My horse carrying me, and my burro carrying a load, obviously were far more weary and dry than I was. The mountains looming up before me seemed not to get any nearer in spite of added miles of travel. Needed was a camp, but a camp meant water, and water seemed yet to be a remote prospect. Suddenly, I noticed my animals lowering their heads and sniffing the sand, which now had a darker shade and additional vegetation. It was moisture seeping through the sand. The terrain began to change from desert to low foothills, and soon the welcome sparkle of available water appeared in an actual stream. My animals drank until I had to stop them so they would not founder. Here they also had green fodder, where I hobbled them and pitched my camp.

What a luxury, I thought, to get out of the desert. Whoever

"I rode all day on the desert . . ."

conceived the derogatory term, "desert rat," apparently felt as I had an hour earlier. No doubt, he had been long in the desert and didn't like it. Yet, we have those who dearly love the desert and its eternal sun. Perhaps one learns to love the mountains by traveling all day in the desert. But vice versa?

How, alternatively, on leaving the lush timber, lake, and river country, one learns to love and pleasurably adjust to the desert, I haven't yet discovered. I have been told that one needs to make the adjustment gradually over a substantial period of time. What that period might be, I will most likely never learn, since in the early nineteen-sixties, my wife and I set out to make the effort but eventually failed.

Leaving the North when the temperature was twenty-two degrees below zero, we headed down into the Southwest, hoping to make a compromise with the dryness of the Chihuahuan Desert and a river, the Pecos, that flowed from the Rockies, to cross the desert not far from our adobe cabin door. Annually we would take up residence there for a few months. Perhaps the intrigue we felt was more like that of astronauts coming upon the moon. The desert did fascinate us in a strange sort of way—even to the extent of inspiring a book, *Greenhorns in the Southwest*. Doggedly, we stayed with the dry environment, hoping eventually to make the adjustment. Although a river and an irrigation ditch flowed nearby, the lack of rain was an ever-present pall. "It's a pretty day" was a common expression. One felt in time that it would be "prettier" if the sky would darken and shut out the sun for a single merciful cloudy hour of relief, and saturate the thirsty landscape with a drenching downpour.

Thus, visions of rushing rivers, of tumultuous rapids, of windblown rain on whitecapped lakes were some of the images that danced in our heads. We yearned for the thunderous roar and powerful flow of waterfalls in the Canadian wilds, for forests dense with growth. In our effort to make an adjustment to the desert, we convinced ourselves that the aridity provided a unique system, a whole new phase of nature worth studying. The economy of moisture in various desert plants did seem miraculous in its way of preserving every drop of water through periods when the soil to the bottom of their roots was dry as talcum. We told ourselves that dust storms which kept visibility to a hundred feet were a normal part of the desert to which we should adapt.

So futilely we philosophized and schemed to overcome the effects of sand in cabin door locks and failed to know just what to conclude when, on splitting wood, the grit in the billets of piñon pine sent out sparks from the ax, and the finely-honed edge of the ax began to resemble the teeth of a hacksaw. Eventually, we sold the place to people who had been born and raised in the immediate environment. They loved it. They wondered how we could possibly tolerate the environment in the northern forests, where the sun did not shine at least eighty-five percent of the time.

To analyze the nature of life indigenous to different areas resolves itself into a great deal more than placing the various species in their respective categories. Seeking a reason for one species prospering in a certain environment which another similar species finds unviable could end in some unresolved, nebulous theory. It would be no final or logical answer to the "why?" of adjustment or adaption to an environment. All we would know is that the adjustment had been made, not why the species did not abandon one environment for another which would seem by its greater advantages to make existence more tenable.

There appears to be no logical reason, for example, why the

early Eskimo did not seek a milder climate farther south. Battles with the Indian were fought when the Eskimo strayed below the Arctic, but this can scarcely be the reason attributed to his attachment to the Far North. When later, more peaceful times enabled him to occupy what for him might seem to have been less severe climatic regions farther south, he nevertheless sought the frigid arctic prairie and the far northern coasts for his survival and pleasure. The Franklin Expedition, exploring the Arctic, failed to survive the climatic rigors of the region where the Eskimo was at home—the Eskimo in that environment being perhaps one of the most adapted and happy peoples on earth.

To return to the story about visiting my mountaineer friend, I found myself oscillating between the theory of Stewart Edward White, who found mountains not intimate enough, and my friend's inescapable attachment to them. The cabin, set picturesquely on a mountain stream, could certainly be described in its surroundings as intimate. But my friend also needed, he said, what he saw in the distance from his doorway—great majestic, snowcapped peaks rising into the sky. My wife, having been exposed to Alaska's grand scenery, gets nostalgic for such majesty at times on waking in the morning and not seeing a glacier.

Despite my friend's strong attraction to the mountain wilderness, the desert fascinated him in a mysterious way—his interest punctuated perhaps by the following incident. He had to cross the desert whenever he went to the outside, as I had on coming in. When he first came to these mountains, he concluded that the native Indians had lied to him about the distance to the mountain stream where it came out of the foothills and that they had deliberately sent him into a death trap, because on the desert he came upon the barely discernible re-

"The cabin, set picturesquely on a mountain stream . . ."

mains of a man and a saddled horse. Saddle, packs, muzzle-loading rifle, and a strange side arm, all were so thoroughly disintegrated as to be almost indistinguishable from the dry desert soil. Apparently, the remains had been covered and uncovered repeatedly over many years by the blowing sand.

Carefully, he employed the methods of an archeologist uncovering artifacts, gently brushing away the latest inundating soil. By reason of what he had found, he told himself that he would have to reach water soon, especially for his pack animals and mount. His fears were shortly allayed when to his surprise, he heard the trickle of water and came upon a stream. Had the horseman perished within an hour's travel of life-giving water?

Following the stream at great length, my friend entered the foothills, and in another day, reached the lush, fresh mountains, where he undertook to build his cabin. To himself he muttered an apology to the Indians, and pondered the tragedy which marked the desert trail to his cabin.

By contrast with the "imperiling desert," as he called it, he always found the mountains, on his arrival there, a highly sustaining force.

Reflectively, I see the mountains, the desert, the prairie, and the northern lake, river and forest country with many mixed feelings. As I have been a part of all of them for considerable periods, they have, no doubt, become a part of me. I shun none of them, and return time and time again with a certain nostalgia and profound appreciation for each. Nevertheless, that time has come when the gravitation of interest is stronger for a particular region. I must say, unhesitatingly, that the compelling lure for me is in the great rivers, rockbound lakes, and forests of the North and in the challenging variables of its seasons. There I will, no doubt, be held the adoptive or captive indigene.

The Wilderness Life

An indigenous culture develops, of course, in nearly all areas—people become assimilated to their environment, adjusting to the terrain and adapting to the variables of climate until they would not consider living anywhere else and manifest almost a fear of change. Yet if their offspring happen to leave and take up life in an entirely different environment, a new set of circumstances, the offspring usually make their own adjustment with remarkable facility. It was long ago believed that the Negro was so acclimated to the hot countries that he could not survive in cold regions. Peary went to the North Pole with Matthew Henson, a Negro, and caused stupefaction among those who insisted that Eskimos alone were able to tolerate the arctic blasts. While the Franklin party perished, Stefansson and a number of other explorers went into the same regions and succeeded admirably, living long periods off the country with no serious adverse consequences.

One of the great pastimes is obviously a love for categorizing. We like to put everything in neat, thinkable packages, large or small, and figuratively tie them up with ribbons. A vast amount of pseudoscientific writing purposes to show that the human race and all other species need categorizing to the extent of their belonging in a certain region from which supposedly they have not wandered because of their special innate adaptation. Environment, as we know, alters species over an evolutionary period. Can we believe that by some established order early in nature the species and the environment emerged simultaneously in complement? It doesn't seem so.

What lends a kind of credence to the idea that particular species are selectively complementary to their respective geographical and climatic areas is that certain peoples and creatures appear by nature to be so circumscriptably situated that they cannot live in a different environment. In short, they can make a case for themselves, on apparent rather than actual evidence, as one usually can on every side of every argument. Alternatively, the opposite viewpoint in the established or adapted indigene theory, that we are widely adaptable, can also make a case for itself. What neutralizes the notion that we cannot fully escape our native province is that we have successful migration of various creatures, and dispersal in an ever-increasing flux.

Does the environment make the species, or do the species instinctually choose the environment? We may never know, as we wander, settle, and adapt successfully to just about any environment. Perhaps the behavior expressed by the phrase "territorial imperative" is merely a matter of circumstantial equity, not natural selection. In the meantime the infinitely varied world is a showcase from which we can pick and choose our most desired place to live.

18

Our Place in Nature

JUDGING FROM MAIL RECEIVED from my readers, writing a book dealing variously with wilderness requires that a chapter be devoted to the writer's own concept of man's place in nature. Identifying our place seems to be the query we find most difficult to answer.

A discussion of this subject usually involves us in an endless, nebulous treatment in which we generally "go out the same door that we came in." For that reason there is no intent here to make either a scientific or a conjectural approach to the subject. What I might hope to achieve with a commonplace point of view is to avoid obscurantism and to state what seems obvious in natural phenomena.

"The riddle of the universe" is a phrase that could be uttered aloud without punitive consequences only when freedom of expression and a wide latitude of inquiry about man's apparent place in nature were allowed. One of the strange characteristics in the consideration of man's place in nature, and perhaps the most significant one, is that outside of strictly scientific analysis, man, in his eagerness to account for his place, has shown little curiosity about the billions of years prior to his existence from which his being evolved. His primary concern seems to be how he might perpetually collect existential profits.

What more than a half century of contemplating nature has taught me is that man's limitations—the circumscribed compass of his traits—are always inadvertently manifest in any account of phenomena that he makes. When he attempts some proliferation beyond the scope of these traits, it is generally accomplished at the expense of perverting the most obvious existing conditions of nature. He seems to have a deep aversion to being integral with nature in its most revealing manifestations, and freely indulges in obscurantism to "transcend" whatever his limitations appear to be in the whole pattern of nature.

What we have to presume as a basic hypothesis is that the earth when man first evolved on it held an ecological promise for viable living that has to amaze us beyond any evaluating sense or appreciation we may have given it so far. Somehow we failed to preserve and maintain adequately its most priceless potentials for ourselves and other creatures.

If we could observe and recognize objectively and with a degree of modesty that, of the vast variety of complex fauna which populate the earth, man is, in spite of his self-styled place, only one of the species, we could begin to consider his actual contributions. We could ask what he, as a single species of the mammalian class of vertebrates, has made or done to preserve and maintain the original priceless ecological earth treasure, and what he has done, compared to other species, to depreciate it. As man hopes to exalt himself above all other creatures in the most ennobling sense, what perplexes is that he has not been able to adjust to the earth as well as most other creatures without seriously impoverishing it. Should he not, if he boasts superiority over all other creatures, have striven to make the earth environmentally better in every respect for all life, including his own species?

In our self-adulating defense we usually purport that man *has* improved the earth's viability for himself. To qualify this, we would need to give here a long treatise on his ecological achievements and failures. Since space would hardly allow this, we have to ask more generally, "Is our world today, because of man's place in it, environmentally as good as, better than, or worse than it was at some earlier stage of human development?" Here we are likely to become impaled on the horns of a dilemma from which we will not readily escape. We tend to revere, above viability, accumulated artificial accretions as the marks of improvement.

If we can draw a conclusion: From his origin to his present place man has manifested those limited traits which he as one species has innately and which typify him—certainly no more. These traits will allow him to be exalted only to the degree that his acts of improving or ravaging his environment have demonstrated. If we disagree with those who say that he has been "a worse predator and ravager than all other species on earth," then it should be a simple matter to qualify our opinion by saying that the results of his acts have been good and ecology has not been impaired. In short, the world is better environmentally by virtue of man's predominance. Is it? Certainly it offers greater utilitarian advantages to man. Can he have this utility and still maintain an ecological balance? We may feel sure that he could if he would attach equal importance to both.

Could it be that when man finds his proper place in nature he will be indispensable to the viability and preservation of the earth? While there is a vast disagreement on the merit of man's enterprise as it fosters the welfare of the earth's present and future viability, perhaps we should generously say that he has not yet moved the pieces around so that they fit into a perpetually functional or ecologically stable whole. Is he innately capable of achieving this harmonious relationship with nature, or will the natural forces themselves eventually have to move man into his appropriate place, whatever that might prove to be? This last, I hasten to say, is a speculation on which we cannot afford to rest our future at the risk of extinction.

One scientist has endeavored to show that man's place on earth is relatively insignificant, that the world will eventually be taken over by insects. He shows this battle for equitable control over the planet to be already under way. Man wins a battle now and then with insecticides, he says; but the insects will inevitably win in the end, since insects have been building up a tolerance to the environment and an improved vigor greater than their enemies', and have developed a survival tolerance for insecticides.

A psychology professor once asked his class, as an experiment, what their reaction would be to a "devil's advocate" hypothesis that the earth might someday go on with its many competing species when man had finally become extinct. The general reaction among the students was one of arrogant anthropocentrism. The thought that "inferior" creatures should be allowed the prestigious position now held by man inevitably brought a reaction of anger. Can we presume, therefore, that the position man has arrogated to himself down through history simply is the result of naïvely hoping to exalt his own position above all other natural phenomena?

Man fought wilderness. He has tried to rise ecologically above his place in it. But did he, in his fight, truly consider the merit of destroying the wilderness principally to manifest his superiority over other creatures, over ecology as a predominating, balancing force greater than his own which might exact a terminal penalty if he did not observe its essentials?

If we could choose the periods in history in which we would prefer to live, it is very likely that all of the past, the present, and the future would be more or less equally represented; due to our individual capriciousness of choice, each era would seem to be the greatest era in which man has a place. There is, we find, much nostalgia for the past and a certain hope for the future. There seems to be a moot attitude toward the present. If I were to appraise my own contemporary period, I would suggest that it is certainly the most *transitive* of all past periods, and possibly exceeds what could appear as possible transitivity in the future. For example, I saw the wilderness early in the century when it was far less invaded and ravaged. I saw the peak of industrial development rise and an incidental population about to reach a saturation point. I think that I am also entering that transitory period when we are beginning to amend, when as the result of a new consciousness we will try to set the natural world right again.

Obviously, man has not yet fully found his place in nature, or managed a viable adjustment to it. It is remotely possible that for the first time in his history, he is *beginning* to find his place, though slowly. From recent discoveries of cause and effect, he knows he has no choice but to find it. If that place means turning things back or into a harmonious relationship with nature, is it not true that man had much greater opportunity to curb the burgeoning menace to ecology earlier in his development? Now belatedly he ponders, and I think seriously, how he can push back the confusion of utilitarian "progress" and overpopulation to a state where his existence comes into harmony with nature.

It would appear that the most basic element needed for man to accomplish this harmony is the tempering of his self-exaltation as it concerns his proper place in nature. It seems quite obvious that he needs to arrive at that point of rationalization where he finds every creature, every plant, every grain of soil, every drop of water, every breath of air on earth, in its chemistry, its physics, the miracle of its existence, just as important a phenomenon as he is. If we deride this fact, let us realize that we evolved from these very elements and obviously will return to those same elements from which we sprang, as will every other living thing.

To have looked upon all other life as *lower* than man, no doubt, is part of the ecological setback from which man now suffers. The earth beneath our feet, the air, sun, and rain, are the elements that will form the generations that will replace us. If in our false pride we desecrate the earth in any manner, we desecrate potential mankind and other life to come. From the vibrant earth, which we tend to pronounce *inert matter,* will come great and beautiful people, domestic and wild life, forests, and bloom. The silent life of earth, if we could hear it stirring in the elements beneath our feet, in the air, and in the chemistry of light, would be an almost frightening potential to contemplate, most likely greater than anything we have conceived in the past or that exists in the present.

We tend to think of the billions of people, animals great and small, and plant organisms now living as permanent entities. They will, in the province of time, pass; and from the earth's so-called "inert" matter shall spring the elements for the life to come. The mass of life now existing, including human life, will be physically and chemically component of that life to come.

We point at times to the miracle of man in contrast with what we have been told to regard as the lower life forms. I have often been amazed at the miracle of sight, the whole complex system that makes up the eye, and its relation to light. It is easy to see how in our self-adulation we might want to give greater value to man's sight than to the sight of all other creatures. But man does not have the optical capability of an eagle, for example, or of some insects. Man's olfactory organs are better than a few creatures' and infinitely worse than most. And so we could go on making comparisons, sense by sense, with endless futility, always hoping that we can exalt ourselves above all other life. Why must we make the derogatory comparison? To the superior characteristics of animals other than man we apply the term "instinct"; these same qualities in man we attribute to "intelligence."

The insect, the fence post, the leaf, and whatever organic matter have decayed and formed the chemistry assimilated perhaps centuries ago or a season ago by the earth's processes may become a part of the chemistry that will be the human prodigy, the fool, or a soaring eagle a hundred or a thousand years from now. Why then disassociate ourselves from a single atom beneath our feet, and disturb the ecology that will transmute it to the living form? What is the purpose of presuming for dignity's sake alone that human life is dearer than all other forms of life in the cosmic whole? Can we not exalt all life without losing our own prestige? Are we not a constituent of the whole?

If through compelling circumstance and increased knowledge we finally manage to enter into a harmonious relationship with nature, it seems we will have an urgent need to edit or

delete much of our documented self-adulating conjecture. We
have to see ourselves in the light of the best possible intellectual
honesty that we can project into the present and ascending
ecological pattern. That happens to be recognition of our own
integral, indissoluble link with all life.

We might ask most personally, would we defile those atoms
that might some day be part of our own progeny? Atomically,
could they diversely derive from the rain that will fall, the
residue of bloom that once withered, a feather that falls from
the sky? I often wonder what conglomerate elements over
billions of years were finally metamorphosed into my own
being.

American Indians, earlier, left their dead suspended high on
wooden scaffolds, presuming rightfully that their ancestors'
elements would be transmuted into the trees that grew, into
the "voice of the rapids." The Indian says, "I am the earth, a
whole person, not a part of a person, nor a part of the earth.
I am the essence of what the earth is."

We need profoundly to think about this.

Is the American Indian's concept absurd? If we are of the
same chemical composition as the material that is around us,
then it is obvious that by transmutation we have been formed
by a collection of these elements, as the American Indian pro-
claims, "the essence of what the earth is."

What is puzzling, of course, is that any creature, whether it
be ourselves or the eagle soaring above us, besides being of the
earth's elements, has animation which we call life. The chemistry of our bodies, which is about ninety-five percent water
and five percent the earth's vibrant solid matter, needs to be
animated if we are to see the spectacle or miracle we view as a
living being. But the eagle, the mouse, the insect, the weed,

the bacterium—no matter how we propose to differentiate—the organisms of the earth have that thing called *life* as well.

Of course, the very tiny atoms or molecules that compose all matter are in themselves alone just as vibrant with life as are living beings, whether the matter is a part of our living bodies or what we see as "inert" material. We can, therefore, look as astounded upon the vibrant atom or molecule as we look upon animated organisms, which include man.

It is, therefore, just as perplexing to understand the vibrant life of the atom and molecule as it is to comprehend the animation of living organisms. But here we seem *not* to be satisfied that the link between vibrant matter and living beings is the same in human beings as it is in the soaring eagle, the insect, or the creature that grazes to become our protein diet. Is obscurantism our only safe human retreat from all other life? Life per se exists in *all* creatures.

In many respects our senses, of course, permit more comprehension than do those of our fellow creatures, while in many respects our senses are seriously inferior to theirs. Therefore, sense variance is a matter of both lower and higher degree, depending on how we go about making a comparison.

Do we conclude from these variances above and below the level of the human mind that the human being supersedes in every way all that is evident in nature?

We get back to the proposition that the indicted purport to be their own jurists. As animals generally assume a territorial imperative, so does man. The difference is that man, in his anthropocentricity, has little tolerance and regard for the rights of other species in their respective territories. Man feels that he has the prerogative to invade the territories of any or all other species, and to displace those species with whatever he chooses to impose of his own, to whatever end of devastation. One might excuse this on a primitive survival-of-the-fittest premise, except that a too heavy-handed usurpation tends, as we are rapidly discovering, to rebound ecologically and to seriously depreciate the role of the victorious invader, if he does not risk eliminating himself entirely.

19

Wilderness Destiny

A few months before writing these lines, I returned from a number of pontoon plane flights over some of the wildest regions of the North American continent. It was a nontechnical, perfunctory survey of personal interest which may not be directly pertinent to these pages, except that the result of the observations might be valuable information for those readers who are apprehensive about the shrinkage of the contemporary wilderness and about the chances for preserving it for the future.

As to a wilderness remaining, let us say here at once that those concerned readers can take much encouragement. So extensive and wild are most of the wilderness-encompassed lakes and rivers—hundreds of thousands of them—in the provinces east and west of Hudson Bay, that a canoe voyager will be able to cover only a relatively small segment of the waterways in his most vigorous life-span. The province of Ontario alone is said to have about one hundred thousand or more lakes—most wild, bound up with a vast network of connecting rivers. If the challenge is yet not great enough, then the districts of Mackenzie and Keewatin should overwhelm the most ambitious. Alaska boasts a similar pattern. The wilderness potential is equally great where the mountains, packhorse, and backpack country is concerned.

Perhaps the reader will jump to the conclusion that because the country I covered was traversed by airplane, it will in time be as readily overrun by plane. Of all means of wilderness travel, I can say advisedly that plane flight offers its passengers the least intimate contact with the wilderness and fewer inroads than we might think. I might add that the snowmobile incursion is in much the same category. This does not say that these vehicles are not expeditious means of conveyance into the wilds. The point is that the plane is very transient. When it reaches the wilds, it pauses momentarily and is gone. By its inherent properties, it cannot economically or practically remain in the wilds for extended periods unless service-based for maintenance. What we have to consider is that once such modes of travel have brought the wilderness traveler to remote places, he has to depart from such mechanization in favor of quiet, local travel if he is to glean those values from the wilds which are his very reason for being in a wilderness area. Proof of this is to try individually using the various vehicles and means of travel—be it plane, snowmobile, dog team, hand-hauled toboggan, canoe, packhorse, or simply backpacking. As in the relationship between man and woman, only intimacy with wilderness can achieve results.

Some will presume that in traveling by one of the more rudimentary forms of transportation, such as canoe, packhorse, or backpacking, planes overhead will be disturbing. This is perhaps more psychological than actual, since the hum of a bush-type plane high overhead is scarcely audible, and the momentary sight of it no more imposing than the sight of a soaring eagle. A woodsman of long standing remarked to me that planes used for travel in the wilderness were primarily for restless people, or for making a quick freight haul. Their passengers come, and before they have made the least adjustment, or imposed harmful incursion upon a wild area, they are gone. Their "comprehensive" report on reaching the outside world, however, has at times been, "I have covered every square inch of that country," which might be considered comparable to studying natural history at an elevation of two thousand feet at plane speed, and identifying the various individual species.

One need only fly over the most remote part of the North American wilderness to learn how small an insect a plane can be. Should it, by some mechanical failure, crash deep in the forest, the chances are that it might never be found. Since I had a desire to document much of my flight over the wilderness, I did the navigating for the pilot, and derived a great deal more comfort from a sextant and the government's tabulated solutions of the spherical triangle than from any confidence I had that, if we were irreparably grounded, we would eventually be found. One hopes, of course, in the event of mechanical failure in the air with a pontoon-equipped plane, that a glide can be made to a water surface—a feat not always possible.

Perhaps one of the great momentary thrills of the trip was to be set down in a plane on a substantial wilderness lake and know that the waters were washing a shore without a human being on it. What made the pleasure brief was, of course, the singular distraction of having the plane to consider.

Now and then, the pilot and I were able while aloft to identify a body of water from its general shape, but this neces-

"I . . . derived a great deal more comfort from a sextant . . ."

sitated a very high altitude observation. Largely, if our position was uncertain, we found it best to set down on the lake and taxi onto some shore for a noon observation on the sun to get a latitude line of position, or to make two observations on the sun at substantial intervals, for a fix to obtain an exact position. Every night in camp when the sky was clear we "shot the stars," to verify our exact position.

A nostalgic reaction naturally was experienced in flying over routes which much earlier I had traveled by canoe, packhorse, or on foot. To note that the region was apparently as wild now as it had been when first my canoe touched the many shores, was to gather further assurance that much of the wilderness still remains inviolate.

Another illusion, as indicated, for those concerned about "nuisance" travel vehicles over the wilds, is to presume that when winter comes, snowmobiles will be crisscrossing the wilderness, destroying its solitude. It might be of interest to the concerned that a very small percentage of snowmobiles ever get into the deeper wilds. Other than those used by wilderness natives and officials, most snowmobiles are used for racing and general gamboling over open snow areas and road ditches in and near towns. Those snowmobiles which do reach the outlying woods from towns most frequently are found on such trails in semi-wild country as have been developed by the conservation agencies of states and provinces for snowmobiles. Idealistically, as snowmobilers we propose to equip ourselves with camp gear and set out into the remote wilderness areas to camp, travel, and see the far interior of the wilderness. The comparatively few who do generally have a favorable attitude that supports the wilderness, along with competence and high regard for solitude, which makes them a pleasure to see.

Many of the long winter journeys, despite the snowmobile,

are still being made by dog team. It is not wise to make a long trek into the wilderness with only one snowmobile, whereas with only a dog team it can be done with a high margin of continual success. Mechanical breakdown of the snowmobile is too common. Two or more such units are needed as a safety factor, and even then the survival method should be to trail a hand-haul type of toboggan behind the snowmobile with camp equipment and an ample food supply. The hand-hauled type of toboggan should be used rather than the commercial type of snowmobile trailer, which does not lend itself very well to hand-hauling.

"Give me just a bone," said the dilettante anthropologist, "and I will reconstruct the whole animal." To presume what the destiny of the wilderness will be is perhaps to become as conjectural as this. The difference in the two hypotheses, however, is that we have more than the bone to go on. There is a grand, natural world remaining on which to begin our program of improved living. The short road to human disaster, of course, would be to risk destroying this remaining wilderness potential.

It may be that we will in time develop the much needed awareness and reverence for wilderness values. A man told me that he has raked leaves by the hundreds of millions in his yard for years every fall, and until he retired he never thought to examine a single one to note the intricate beauty of its veinal pattern, to say nothing of investigating its unique and miraculous natural life function on the growing tree. Where are the people who used to press autumn leaves in books?

There is a tendency to be pessimistic about the future of the wilderness, the pessimists considering that apprehension, if stressed enough, would increase positive general concern. I rise each morning believing that the tide *has* turned and that wilderness is now and will be recognized, finally, as "the preservation of the world."

Have we actually changed our minds about wilderness? Not, perhaps, through a sufficient understanding of the need to avert impending disaster, but largely by stumbling pell-mell over our ecological blunders and having the good sense to regain our footing and walk more competently upright.

Many of us are now apparently resolved on a program of preserving what we have. In the past we saw only a world of unlimited natural resources. We tended to forget the basic origin from which things emanated. This was because conventional life was so far removed from natural phenomena. Scarcely ever did we get down to regarding the actual wilderness resources which produced the thing in hand. Lumber came from the orderly rack in the lumberyard. There was little reflection that it derived from a limited number of trees of a certain species, growing precariously in a particular threatened area, that might have significance in the whole ecological framework of human life. There was little thought to preserving forests for perpetual cultivation. Increasing the board feet of lumber on hand was the order of the day, not the potential of perpetual forest growth and cultivation.

In time we may come not only to see wilderness as enterprise, but to be so aware of it as to see the vibrant, colorful beauty of the morning sun refracted in a drop of water clinging to a spider web by capillary attraction. To do this we obviously require leisure—a pause in our economic fretfulness.

If we become aware of origin, of basics, of natural phenomena, of wilderness in essence, it will probably be because our understanding of ecologic interdependence is telling us that human survival is hopeless without it, and that optimum living is possible with it.

One can be hopeful. The forces of nature will inevitably, of course, win in the end, no matter what our course. Of that we may be sure. What we need now is to be self-sustaining and magnanimous at the same time; in short, save the wilderness that exists for our own immediate need and enjoyment, and project a permanent pattern for future generations to follow.

How can we go about it? A single congressional session of fearless legislation would be worth one hundred years of political, office-gaining rhetoric. Public zeal that floods the politician's desk with letters would do it. He fears most of all his political demise.

We need to determine conclusively, in any program, where the metropolis must establish its limits, and where the natural environment, indispensable to both city and country life, should begin. Most important is that we have enough wisdom to know when our industries have reached that point beyond which there are only rapidly diminishing returns for mankind and the environment.

Having enjoyed more than a half century of living a large part of each year in the wilderness, and by virtue of it having lived close to manual processes, I am inclined to regard many of the mechanized devices of modern life as not so tragically dispensable should they suddenly become unavailable or greatly reduced in number through energy shortage or some other unforeseen condition. Much of the seeming indispensability of the goods of modern living is mere illusion gained from nefarious advertising, or from consumers succumbing to convenience gadgets that permit a physically phlegmatic life. We could become a stronger people by having less. We could become nobler by improving our sense of personal and national economy, avoiding all kinds of needless waste of resources.

The prevalent truancy from the establishment has pointed up

an increasing need for our industrial society to find a life-style different from that which we have to date so passionately pursued. For a while I thought the sudden economic and social rebellion was only a fad of the young—a revolt symbolized by long hair, beards, and faded, patched blue jeans—until I found executives, professionals, and others in no small number leaving their briefcases behind and breaking down the conventional barbed wire to get some relief from an artificially circumscribed life.

Within the time span of a few months, we have seen power companies pass through a transition from spending fortunes on advertising that would induce increased use of energy, to inverse advertising persuading us to use less. This has to be considered the industrial paradox of our time.

We can hope that industrial incursion upon the natural areas will, by virtue of this paradoxical change, tend somewhat to decrease. Those who saw the globe ultimately surfaced with asphalt may now be able to quell at least their worst fears. The integrating natural forces, I am inclined to believe, will gradually have a better chance in the amending processes, especially if legislation can be passed that will prevent ravage from running wild.

We have reached a point when we are benefiting by much of the technology that was possible when we had an abundance of fuel energy and basic materials on which to splurge research. It may be that we will now begin to level off by a process of limitation and critical refinement in which we utilize and can enjoy the best of the technology already acquired. This is well within the realm of achievement if we require maximum quality in everything we make to replace the plethora of ephemeral trash. It is just possible that we can discover a life-style better characterized by the term "quality" than by "repletion."

As a pebble dropped into the water affects the entire pond with waves, so have we seen the recent energy and other shortages ramify into every human endeavor, man's encroachment on the wilderness being no exception. Industry that threatened to make reckless incursions upon the wilderness is, thus, very likely to be encouragingly cut back.

Moderating industrial and social excesses could bring many advantages. It could tend to improve the health of the populace, cause avarice to slack off, to make current living less materialistic. We might hope that it would reduce the decibel count of raucous noise, and even offer a measure of urban tranquility. There may be fewer trips to the obtrusively mounting dumps if we employ recycling processes more universally. Sentiment might be attached to a material thing if quality became the dominant measure of value. The upgrading in quality of our actual life-style as well might catch on so admirably that the stranger to us on the sidewalk might acquire a countenance of hope and cheer to replace his look of apprehension or despair.

Many of us have been too busy to plant a garden: besides, it was not thought "economically feasible." We may see fit to do it now for pleasure, as physical and mental therapy, and, with mounting food costs, even for profit. If ten million will be unemployed because of the energy shortage, or because we have begun to make less trash and more quality goods, possibly we can re-employ them if we all work ten percent fewer hours. The word "overtime" may soon become archaic; at least, it should be regarded as a disgraceful concept in a life of underemployment and lack of leisure.

I cannot believe that we are so technologically incompetent that we have to suffer a deteriorating life-style if there is a drastic shortage of fuel for energy. Nor will I believe that even with adequate energy it is necessary to destroy the oceans, rivers, and lakes of the world in order to sustain an economically stable living standard. It has become obvious—and we hope mandatory—that we will have to allocate a substantial portion of our energy to cleaning up what we dirty up in the industrial process.

Almost as suddenly as the emergence of our awareness of the fuel shortage, there appeared a trend toward a decreasing birthrate in our own and a number of other countries, which may prove to be the cardinal need. Hospitals have recently had to reduce the size of their maternity wards. What should be apparent, to all of us who hear projections and those of us who attempt to make them, is that wherever there is an action there is also a reaction—a strong, controlling, basic principle in nature to consider. Growth in both animal and vegetable life wherever it becomes excessive kills itself off, thus moderating itself. We have an example in the wilderness cycle in which overriding populations of rodents bring on a large population of carnivores. We might suppose that a population explosion of both rodents and carnivores would result, which is the wrong supposition. Cyclically, as carnivores increase, rodents decrease; and soon, in turn, the carnivores decrease. We have not been able fully to comprehend what in nature brings about the auto-destructive control of its various species. We attribute it to a lack of sufficient food or growth-promoting elements, but this does not reveal all the cyclical factors.

We are satisfied with nature's control processes until they apply to the human species. Something in the dignity or anthropocentricity of man repels the basic notion about nature's process of self-reduction where the human race is concerned. What we need to reflect on is that the human species has, no doubt, cyclically increased and decreased for countless years. Had there been no natural laws periodically controlling his number, there would have been "standing room only" on earth many centuries ago. Fears that a population explosion to the point of standing room only might happen today or in the not too distant future become absurd as soon as we study nature's controlling cycle of animal and plant life. When excessive populations make life untenable, there will be, we can be sure, a natural, automatic cutback. What seems tragic about this is that nature's impersonal need to decimate large populations would not occur if man had the wisdom to keep the number of his own species in bounds, the means being now available to him.

We are on the other hand warned that the human species might become an endangered one. Nothing foreseeable portends this although other species have become extinct, sometimes as a result of man's activities, and man is certainly threatening the decimation of his own kind more than seems to be natural if we look at the auto-destruction cycle in other creatures

We can assume that as fossil energy fuels diminish, the population might proportionately diminish to where it will have the most ideally viable combination of natural and industrial conditions ever experienced by man. Perhaps Winston Churchill was right when he said in essence that the internal combustion engine was a curse to humanity. When most fossil fuels have been used up, the population will inevitably fall back on those remaining kinds of energy which do not threaten the ecology of the earth: various types of water power, geothermal energy, and, perhaps most of all, solar energy. But we may also see a great revival in manual energy—a force that diminished rapidly when other energy was harnessed and consequently left the majority of people physically weaker. Who could have predicted twenty-five years ago that cities would now need to provide bicycle lanes along paved automobile roads?

We are haunted by the concept that as industrial progress is made, wilderness has to suffer in direct ratio. The hopeful prospect that we might have an accelerating scientific achievement with an improvement of our environment seems incredible to many. But, to repeat, *quality* is the civilizing term—not repletion. An improved civilization could be had by a reverse of those factors which heretofore brought a combination of industrial gain and environmental debasement.

We can, however, be impressed with the recent growing ecological awareness that is filtering into every department of human endeavor. While to the individual and the minority belong the laurels for this growing awareness, we can have much encouragement in Lincoln's advisement that "The mind of the minority becomes the mind of the majority." And an aroused public, in the final analysis, has usually brought about the major change.

20

A Retrospective Glance

THE MAN WHO blazed the near side of trees with an ax along his outbound route through the forest, found on his return that he had no visible blazed trail to follow.

Our perspective early in life can be much like that. Our eyes are focused forward. We seem to be inexorably bound up with the future, presuming that the new should hold the chief interest, the old holding just hollow criteria, although retrospection can hold future's guide. Our steps are seldom considered profitably retraceable. Someone suggested that if we were capable of taking life's routine back, most of what we had observed would be different. What we had seen on the forward trail would on our return be seen from a wholly different angle. Obviously, there is wisdom in this, if it can be proposed that both sides of any issue or the forward route and back trail of travel tend to be equally edifying and revealing.

The *retrospective glance* into our past should tell us that some things might have been regarded as highly favorable, while others could have been dispensed with to the best advantage in life's pursuit. But foresight does not have quite this comprehensiveness. We tend to make our wisest value judgments belatedly on what the past has taught us.

This can apply as well to those who have reached the pinnacle of success. It has been said in disparagement that when you reach the top there is no place to go.

There *is* a place to go. The likelihood looms large that you once were already there; all you need do in order to arrive again is retrace your steps. This may need qualification.

An immediate single example of many is the late Chet Huntley. As one of the nation's top reporters, his newsbeat took him into just about every niche and cranny of life. It can be said that he knew from long urban contact the din and the glare of the cities. As he stated more generously, he had heard the "music of the metropolis," although he did not tell us how traumatic he found each day, or if the decibel level was too screechingly high to lend a full ear. He had, nevertheless, ascended the higher peaks of broadcasting, until one day, scanning the world on the dizzying peaks of success, he had to make a decision; he had to go somewhere.

He went to Big Sky, a wilderness region in Montana which he owned and converted into a recreational area. When he was interviewed about this, he recalled the naturalistic values of his youth, which he found in the grandeur of the Big Sky country. Perhaps he should have gone sooner to Big Sky, for he was to revel happily in his wilderness sanctuary only about four years until, to the whole nation's loss, death took him.

There is a temptation at this point to mention the names and give pertinent biographical sketches of many prominent people who reached the top and still found *a place to go*. It is better, perhaps, to make generalizations. A commendable thing about many highly accomplished and prominent career people is that they choose not to keep going at what they are doing until they "die with their boots on." What they accomplish at the peak of their achievement is to leave it and seek those natural areas of their childhood where tomorrow's dawn breaks as though for the first time in history truth and beauty were discovered.

In short, they seek to re-create what they actually possessed before they were motivated to climb to the pinnacle of success. Having finally arrived in the cold, rarified atmosphere of the peaks, they long for the warm, lush green valley where life may come closest to an experience of euphoria.

At the close of the Second World War, I asked a soldier who had been long in active service what he was going to do when he reached home. Since he had a master's degree in his profession and was the son of affluent parents, I expected his answer would be a rather conventional one of how he would plunge into the busy world and achieve whatever prominence his talents would allow. Instead, he said, "I'm going down to the corner drugstore and have a big malted milk; then I'm going fishing for a long time." And that, I might add, is exactly what he did—with me, although with some modification as to mere fishing. Some of the simpler things in life, we may rightly presume, can be more happily engaging.

On one occasion my wife and I participated in a writers' convention for a week where I was a sponsored guest speaker. We had a magnificent suite of rooms and the finest of fare in an elegant hotel, where the orchestra played and vocal celebrities sang. On the fifth evening, rather late, we took a walk, leaving the splendor of the setting. We walked a mile and came to a tiny greasy-spoon lunch counter. There we each ordered a cup of coffee and a doughnut. The coffee was rank and the doughnuts had a rancid smell. But we consumed both at the risk of indigestion, loitered for a short while, and went back to the luxury of our hotel, our "souls" cleansed of the sins of voluptuousness for the moment. It was perhaps an act of mortification; perhaps we felt the need to wear a hair shirt. The total cost of the two cups of rank coffee and rancid doughnuts was forty cents. We tipped the waiter a dollar. He looked at us bewildered as we smiled and left.

This was *not* a religious penance. We had simply suffered ennui. In short, we were satiated and needed a raw-boning, a revitalizing; as Robert Service put it, we needed "a whiff of bacon and beans, a snug shakedown in the snow."

There is, needless to say, magnificent art in architecture, achievement in fine cuisine, great talent in grooming, industrial genius in pretentious automobiles and complex mechanisms, but unless a life steeped in them is balanced with continual vitalization of the mental and physical self, they become "bilious to body and mind." We are hypnotized and obsessed by the things which convention has set before us. We become so extravagantly accoutered we do not know where the furnishings stop and personal splendor begins.

The human being should be so saliently contrasted in his conventional setting that even luxurious inanimate objects are not seen except in the remote obscurity of his background. When, for example, background music is absorbed in the effect of the drama, it can be a great enhancement. If the music predominates, the actors become obscure, the drama sags.

The years late in life roll on much too fast, ever faster as they accumulate in increasing number. Days seem too short, and continually shorter, as they multiplyingly flash by, but not in the sense of routine accomplishment. It is a reverent need for the priceless moment that gives time its disturbing brevity. We need the joy of living optimally, where every natural force is playing on one's being, as multicolored spotlights play on the actor who is exuberant with the joy of assuming his role. That exquisite pleasure of being an integral part of the natural universe, of being in its spotlight, makes one ecstatic about just living.

At this writing, spring is close at hand, and migrant flocks of robins are foraging on the open patches of ground between snowdrifts. It prompts one to consider what one will do when the full vernal splendor breaks over this part of the world. I do not look forward to startling and exciting events. My wife and I could afford, as readily as not, to board a jetliner and span the oceans, going to countries we have not seen. We are not likely to. It isn't that we believe masonry to be tyrannous, or that tourism is a joining of the peripatetic mob. The extraordinary architecture that solves urban social problems and withstands earthquakes; the plush-seated, air-conditioned motor car that whisks one along the nation's highways; the luxurious café where the world's most tasteful, epicurean delights are served; the fashion shows and shops where the most expensive fine feathers are offered; these, and a thousand other magnificent accomplishments of a busy world, we have admired, praised, coveted when we could not afford some of them, basked and luxuriated at times when we were able to.

But ennui can become a component of luxuriousness. Retrospectively, we see many luxuries as the momentary alleviation of doldrums; others as palliatives for social ills; still others as only meager chances, as Goethe said, to win "liberty afresh each day." They are, no doubt, essential to our kind of society. If we could add to them for the happiness of others, we would. Yet, there comes a time when one runs away from the noisy round of banquets to eat the crust of bread in solitude.

The Wilderness Life

On looking back, one recalls the changes in one's life-style that occur when there is an habitual response to nature. It is the process of getting away from the self and more than anything, from the material. Objectivity in the natural pursuit plays a bigger role. Egocentricity that tends to obtrude upon others fades like the fog in sunlight.

It is not the deciding urgency of the moment, I find, that determines our best conduct. It is the accumulation of what higher consciousness we have gathered in the better environments and with individual association over the years. Too gregarious, we tend to "level with the crowd." That level in the most gregarious sense is scarcely ever upward. A world too busy to raise the cultural level of society above mediocrity is the misfortune of the individual. The leisure required by the individual in a solitary search for cultural values has to be compared with what he gains in trying to achieve some advantage culturally by association with the crowd; for to become overly sensitive to the crowd is often to lose one's sensitivity to the earth's phenomena.

There is a common tendency to have the same purview of nature as we have in our purview of the crowd. Big crowds and the events that pertain to them tend to be equated with the spectacular: great waterfalls, light-explosive sunsets, the Grand Canyon, the stupendous ephemeral bloom of the desert after a heavy rain, rather than to the intrinsic natural values. All of us, of course, respond to natural spectacles. But we might hope that the response would be just as inspired if it were the result of intimately observing a clump of marsh marigolds growing in the spring water near a footbridge or a columbine in the cleft of mossy rocks; and in the same sense should we not be more inclined to value the prodigiousness of the individual than the propriety of the crowd? Does not the individual provide the whole public image?

It is a mistake, of course, to regard the crowd as a separate entity. Break it up into components and variously you find individuals. The important thing, if I may use an analogy, is to remove the valuable jewel from the detraction of its setting wherever you can, and examine its facets separately.

We are sometimes taken to task by convention and asked, "What can you and your wife possibly do up there in the wilderness for months on end? Are you paying some penance for your antisocial attitude?"

"We keep fairly busy," I say. "We take canoe trips, write books, study natural history, try to develop our aesthetic sense by observation and photography, study wildlife, read, indulge in a little astronomy. I practice my celestial navigation in order to travel in the wilder regions, make meteorological observations, dabble a bit in archeology, anthropology, and some of the other sciences, practice woodcraft. We pick berries, gather and cut wood for a stove and fireplace, harvest wild rice with the Indians when they arrive, carry water, listen to the radio, cook and eat, keep house, rest, contemplate the beauty of nature, and, of course, entertain our friends who drop in by canoe, plane, snowmobile or dogsled."

To this recital the answer is often classic in its brevity. "Oh."

We wonder what we would have done differently if we could retrace our steps. Those who visit us at our home "back in civilization" for the first time look for some wilderness theme dominant in our household. The discovery that wilderness on the contrary is an all-embracing subject, as evidenced by the great diversity of our library and our furnishings, is revealing to some, confusing and sometimes even disappointing to others. Those who visit us at our residences on the wilderness fringe and deep in the wilderness find the environment awesome, even at times frightening, if they have been too urbanized, or find it highly engaging if they are of the outdoor fraternity.

On looking back it might be said that we have been doing just about the same thing that other people are doing everywhere, only that we have tried to do it from what we believe to be the best possible vantage point. If, as I have indicated, we are all natural beings, then it would seem that we could not function to the best advantage other than concomitantly as we have with nature's processes.

If I might be allowed, on the basis of my more than three score and ten years of reflection, to make a bold prediction for the future, it is to say that we human beings will have but a minimal part in the final determination of what the elemental world will be. We are obviously living on a finite planet. We have refused to accept its limitations and have looked in the past to science for infinite possibilities. What science has subsequently discovered, in much hypothesizing about infinity, is that we are destined to operate within definable limits—limits which we did not see before, that loom apparent each day. We seem to be getting close to that point where even measurement of the definable limits may be a possibility, proving to be the new science for better living.

What this amounts to is that the world's limited resources and elemental forces—not man's technological discoveries will eventually dictate the outcome. Technology will merely have to adjust. Man will for a time, of course, continue to be as optimistically rampant as he was able to do with the ready energy and materials available to him in the past, but the best technical knowledge and our most honest rationalization now say that a time will come in the not too distant future when he will have to operate within such definable limits as are preset by the earth's phenomena.

We can presume that basically there are two roads: the one which man proposes to travel and the one which he will inevitably have to travel. If he has enjoyed in the past a high exaltation because of his belief in self-determination alone, let him rather revel in the fact that the forces of nature will ultimately provide him, despite his mistakes, with "the best of all possible worlds."

CALVIN RUTSTRUM (1895–1982) was one of the best-known outdoorsmen of his generation and the author of more than a dozen books on wilderness travel and technique, including *The New Way of the Wilderness, North American Canoe Country, Once upon a Wilderness, Paradise Below Zero,* and *The Wilderness Route Finder,* all published in paperback by the University of Minnesota Press.